| Vaccines

Other Books in the Current Controversies Series

America's Teachers

Assisted Suicide

Developing Nations

Drug Trafficking

Espionage and Intelligence

Gays in the Military

The Global Impact of Social Media

Government Corruption

Illegal Immigration

The Iranian Green Movement

The Middle East

Nuclear Armament

Politics and The Media

Pollution

The Tea Party Movement

The Uninsured

Current
CONTROVERSIES

| Vaccines

Noël Merino, Book Editor

GREENHAVEN PRESS
A part of Gale, Cengage Learning

GALE
CENGAGE Learning·

Detroit • New York • San Francisco • New Haven, Conn • Waterville, Maine • London

Elizabeth Des Chenes, *Managing Editor*

© 2012 Greenhaven Press, a part of Gale, Cengage Learning

Articles in Greenhaven Press anthologies are often edited for length to meet page requirements. In addition, original titles of these works are changed to clearly present the main thesis and to explicitly indicate the author's opinion. Every effort is made to ensure that Greenhaven Press accurately reflects the original intent of the authors. Every effort has been made to trace the owners of copyrighted material.

Cover image copyright © Svanblar/Shutterstock.com.

LIBRARY OF CONGRESS CATALOGING-IN-PUBLICATION DATA

Vaccines / Noël Merino, book editor.
    p. cm. -- (Current controversies)
    Includes bibliographical references and index.
    ISBN 978-0-7377-5640-1 (hardback) -- ISBN 978-0-7377-5641-8 (paperback)
    1. Vaccines--Juvenile literature. 2. Vaccination--Juvenile literature. I. Merino, Noël.
    RA638.V33212 2012
    615.3'72--dc23
                                                                2011052064

Printed in the United States of America
2 3 4 5 6 7 16 15 14 13 12

Contents

Foreword   **11**

Introduction   **14**

Chapter 1: Are Vaccines Effective in the Prevention of Disease?

Overview: Immunity from Disease   **19**
by Vaccination

College of Physicians of Philadelphia

Vaccination works to stimulate an immune response in the body, specific to a particular pathogen, in order to protect against disease from infection by the pathogen.

Yes: Vaccines Are Effective in the Prevention of Disease

Vaccines Are Effective in Preventing   **23**
Many Diseases

National Institute of Allergy and Infectious Diseases

Vaccines prevent disease through individual and herd immunity, and they have successfully eliminated or lessened the occurrence of many diseases.

Many Deadly Diseases Would Return   **29**
If We Stopped Vaccinations

Centers for Disease Control and Prevention (CDC)

Vaccines have reduced or eliminated many diseases, and if immunization against these diseases were stopped, there would be a resurgence of disease.

No: Vaccines Are Not Effective in the Prevention of Disease

There Is Evidence That Vaccines Promote,   **40**
Rather than Eradicate, Disease

Alex Newman

The historical evidence from past vaccination programs undermines the claim by the government that vaccines are safe and effective.

Vaccines Have Not Been Proven   51
to Be Safe or Effective
    Sherri Tenpenny
    Despite the dogma perpetuated by the medical commu-
    nity, vaccine safety and efficacy have not been proven
    and, in fact, there is evidence that vaccines can harm
    rather than protect patients.

There Is Little Evidence That Flu   58
Vaccines Are Effective
    Shannon Brownlee and Jeanne Lenzer
    Because the medical and public-health community re-
    fuses to question the efficacy of flu vaccination, we are
    failing to consider other options for protecting the public
    from the influenza virus, and in so doing are promoting
    a false sense of security based on an illusion.

Chapter 2: Do the Benefits of Vaccines Outweigh Possible Harms?

Overview: Fear of Vaccines   71
    Amanda Gardner
    Fear of vaccines has existed in varying degrees since the
    first vaccine was developed, prompted by the nature of
    immunization and parental concern.

Yes: The Benefits of Vaccines Outweigh Possible Harms

Concerns About Vaccine Safety Are   75
Out of Proportion to Actual Risk
    National Network for Immunization Information
    Many people are uninformed or misinformed about the
    risks of vaccines, and they do not appreciate the greater
    risks posed by foregoing vaccination.

Concerns About a Link Between Vaccines   82
and Autism Are Unfounded
    John E. Calfee
    Despite the widespread worry that vaccines cause autism,
    the main study that fostered this worry has been thor-
    oughly discounted as fraudulent.

**No: The Benefits of Vaccines Do Not
Outweigh Possible Harms**

Vaccines Are a Danger to Health   88
  Russell L. Blaylock
  Despite the advice of prominent medical authorities, vaccines do not effectively protect against disease and can
  actually cause immune suppression, disease, and cancer.

Chapter 3: Should Certain Vaccinations Be Mandatory?

Chapter Preface   102

Yes: Certain Vaccinations Should Be Mandatory

Mandatory Vaccinations with   104
Few Exceptions Are Necessary
for Public Health
  Pediatric Infectious Diseases Society
  States ought to make it very difficult to obtain an exemption from vaccine mandates, since the health of the entire community depends upon widespread immunization.

The HPV Vaccine Should Be a Part   111
of Mandatory School Vaccines
  Ellen M. Daley and Robert J. McDermott
  The HPV (human papillomavirus) vaccine is safe and effective for preventing cervical cancer, so it should be included among the vaccines mandated for school entry.

The Flu Vaccine Should Be Mandatory   117
for Health Care Workers
  Richard F. Daines
  Because they need to give priority to patients' health and
  welfare, health care workers should be mandated to get
  vaccinated against influenza each year.

**No: Certain Vaccinations Should Not
Be Mandatory**

Mandatory Vaccinations Are a Violation   121
of Parental Rights
  Christopher Klicka

Because vaccinations have been shown to harm some children and because parents have the right and responsibility to protect the welfare of their children, states must not mandate vaccinations, but instead must allow parents to choose whether or not to vaccinate.

The HPV Vaccine Should Not Be a Part   128
of Mandatory School Vaccines

Gail Javitt, Deena Berkowitz,
and Lawrence O. Gostin

Because too many unanswered questions remain about the HPV (human papillomavirus) vaccine and because the disease it treats is so different from those addressed by other mandated vaccines, it should not be included as part of the mandatory school vaccine program.

The Flu Vaccine Should Not Be Mandatory   141
for Health Care Workers

David Isaacs and Julie Leask

Without proof of effectiveness, harmlessness, feasibility, and lack of alternatives, the right to choose argues against vaccine mandates for health care professionals.

Chapter 4: What Are Some Key Issues Regarding Vaccine Development Worldwide?

Overview: The Future of Vaccines   146

College of Physicians of Philadelphia

Vaccine researchers are attempting to create new vaccines, as well as achieve higher effectiveness, lower cost, and better delivery of existing vaccines.

An AIDS Vaccine Is Possible and Must   151
Be a Global Effort

International AIDS Vaccine Initiative (IAVI)

Development of an AIDS vaccine is challenging, but even a vaccine that is partially effective, when administered to a large segment of the population, would help in the fight against the spread of HIV and AIDS.

More Money Is Needed for Vaccines   156
for Pandemic Flu

Gary S. Becker

The likelihood of a major flu pandemic, coupled with the possible economic impact, supports spending more money now to stockpile vaccines and antiviral drugs.

Decisions About How to Combat Pandemic Flu Need to Be Restrained   **160**

Henry I. Miller

The reaction to the H1N1 flu in 2009 illustrates that responding to such outbreaks entails difficult decisions, such as whether to rush development of a vaccine, and that governments need to act with judgment and restraint.

Organizations to Contact   **163**

Bibliography   **168**

Index   **175**

Foreword

By definition, controversies are "discussions of questions in which opposing opinions clash" (*Webster's Twentieth Century Dictionary Unabridged*). Few would deny that controversies are a pervasive part of the human condition and exist on virtually every level of human enterprise. Controversies transpire between individuals and among groups, within nations and between nations. Controversies supply the grist necessary for progress by providing challenges and challengers to the status quo. They also create atmospheres where strife and warfare can flourish. A world without controversies would be a peaceful world; but it also would be, by and large, static and prosaic.

The Series' Purpose

The purpose of the Current Controversies series is to explore many of the social, political, and economic controversies dominating the national and international scenes today. Titles selected for inclusion in the series are highly focused and specific. For example, from the larger category of criminal justice, Current Controversies deals with specific topics such as police brutality, gun control, white collar crime, and others. The debates in Current Controversies also are presented in a useful, timeless fashion. Articles and book excerpts included in each title are selected if they contribute valuable, long-range ideas to the overall debate. And wherever possible, current information is enhanced with historical documents and other relevant materials. Thus, while individual titles are current in focus, every effort is made to ensure that they will not become quickly outdated. Books in the Current Controversies series will remain important resources for librarians, teachers, and students for many years.

In addition to keeping the titles focused and specific, great care is taken in the editorial format of each book in the series. Book introductions and chapter prefaces are offered to provide background material for readers. Chapters are organized around several key questions that are answered with diverse opinions representing all points on the political spectrum. Materials in each chapter include opinions in which authors clearly disagree as well as alternative opinions in which authors may agree on a broader issue but disagree on the possible solutions. In this way, the content of each volume in Current Controversies mirrors the mosaic of opinions encountered in society. Readers will quickly realize that there are many viable answers to these complex issues. By questioning each author's conclusions, students and casual readers can begin to develop the critical thinking skills so important to evaluating opinionated material.

Current Controversies is also ideal for controlled research. Each anthology in the series is composed of primary sources taken from a wide gamut of informational categories including periodicals, newspapers, books, U.S. and foreign government documents, and the publications of private and public organizations. Readers will find factual support for reports, debates, and research papers covering all areas of important issues. In addition, an annotated table of contents, an index, a book and periodical bibliography, and a list of organizations to contact are included in each book to expedite further research.

Perhaps more than ever before in history, people are confronted with diverse and contradictory information. During the Persian Gulf War, for example, the public was not only treated to minute-to-minute coverage of the war, it was also inundated with critiques of the coverage and countless analyses of the factors motivating U.S. involvement. Being able to sort through the plethora of opinions accompanying today's major issues, and to draw one's own conclusions, can be a complicated and frustrating struggle. It is the editors' hope that Current Controversies will help readers with this struggle.

Introduction

> "The history of vaccination against polio-
> virus illustrates some of the challenges
> and controversies faced in the develop-
> ment of a vaccination campaign."

Vaccines were first developed in the late eighteenth century. Their use became widespread during the nineteenth
century, with the first laws passed regarding vaccination. In
the nineteenth century, vaccines for cholera, rabies, tetanus,
typhoid fever, and bubonic plague were developed. Additional
vaccines were produced in the twentieth century, including
those for polio, measles, mumps, and rubella. Since the start
of the twenty-first century the vaccines for human papillomavirus, or HPV, and zoster—commonly known as shingles—
have been developed. Vaccines have been credited with eradicating smallpox and drastically reducing the incidence of polio.
In order to be effective, vaccines must work well against the
targeted bacteria or virus and must be made available to a
large enough segment of the population in a timely fashion.
The history of vaccination against poliovirus illustrates some
of the challenges and controversies faced in the development
of a vaccination campaign.

The poliovirus is highly infectious, spread from person to
person through feces, primarily affecting children under the
age of five. Infection by poliovirus causes poliomyelitis (polio),
a disease of the central nervous system. Although the vast majority of people who become infected do not have any symptoms, in a small percentage of cases the disease can cause irre-
versible paralysis that can result in death. There is no cure for
polio, but the incidence of the disease has dropped dramatically since the inception of the polio vaccine in the 1950s. The
disease was first recognized in 1840 and major polio epidem-

ics occurred throughout the world in the early twentieth century. Today, polio remains endemic in only four countries: Nigeria, India, Pakistan, and Afghanistan.

Polio was eradicated in the Americas by the mid-1990s, but it was not an easy road to eradication. There has always been fear of and resistance to vaccines among a minority segment of the population. Fears of vaccines were vindicated, however, when an early polio vaccine was tainted with live poliovirus, causing dozens of cases of polio and a handful of deaths. Then, in the 1960s, the SV40 virus was found to have contaminated the polio vaccine. The US Centers for Disease Control and Prevention (CDC) reports, "It has been estimated that 10–30 million of the 98 million people who received a polio shot actually received a vaccine that contained SV40."[1] There have been some suggestions that SV40 leads to cancer, but no conclusive evidence on the link has been established. These issues of vaccine safety erode public trust and exacerbate the worst fears about vaccines, creating a barrier to mass vaccination. Eventually, public trust in the poliovirus vaccine was largely regained in the United States, but fears remain elsewhere.

The World Health Organization (WHO) launched the Global Polio Eradication Initiative (GPEI) in 1988 to eradicate polio worldwide. WHO reports, "Polio cases have decreased by over 99% since 1988, from an estimated 350,000 cases in more than 125 endemic countries then, to 1,349 reported cases in 2010."[2] Northern Nigeria is one of the places where polio still remains, at least in part due to a vaccine boycott begun in 2003. As explained in a *PLoS Medicine* article:

> In northern Nigeria in 2003, the political and religious leaders of Kano, Zamfara, and Kaduna states brought the immu-

1. US Centers for Disease Control and Prevention (CDC), "Frequently Asked Questions about Cancer, Simian Virus 40 (SV40), and Polio Vaccine," October 22, 2007. www.cdc.gov/vaccinesafety/updates/archive/polio_and_cancer.htm.
2. World Health Organization (WHO), "Poliomyelitis," Fact Sheet no. 114, October 2011. www.who.int/mediacentre/factsheets/fs114/en/.

nization campaign to a halt by calling on parents not to allow their children to be immunized. These leaders argued that the vaccine could be contaminated with anti-fertility agents (estradiol hormone), HIV, and cancerous agents.

Although the government sent the samples of the vaccine abroad for testing, confirming the safety of the vaccine and showing the boycott to be based on rumor, "the lack of trust among the general population in northern Nigeria about the efficacy of Western medicine remained."[3]

Nigeria's testing rates began to improve, but a polio outbreak in 2009 caused by the vaccine itself was another setback. According to CBS News: "In 2007, health experts reported that amid Nigeria's ongoing outbreak of wild polio viruses, 69 children had also been paralyzed in a new outbreak caused by the mutation of a vaccine's virus."[4] Because the oral vaccine used in Nigeria contains the live poliovirus, there is always a chance of infection. The mutation of the virus in this case caused new worries. Nigeria remains one of the four countries that have not eradicated polio.

These examples from the polio eradication campaign illustrate some of the challenges and controversies involved in vaccination. On the one hand, in order for vaccination to be effective the public needs to trust the vaccines. On the other hand, the public's trust is contingent upon belief in the safety and efficacy of vaccines. There is an ongoing debate about the safety and effectiveness of vaccines, and whether or not their benefits outweigh the risks. A debate rages as well over whether or not vaccinations should be mandatory for children attending public school. In addition, there is disagreement about whether pursuing the development of vaccines is the best way

3. Ayodele Samuel Jegede, "What Led to the Nigerian Boycott of the Polio Vaccination Campaign?" *PLoS Medicine*, March 20, 2007. www.plosmedicine.org/article/info:doi/10.1371/journal.pmed.0040073.
4. CBS News, "Mutant Polio Virus Spreads in Nigeria," August 14, 2009. www.cbsnews.com/stories/2009/08/14/health/main5242168.shtml.

to deal with public health crises. These contentious issues and others are explored in *Current Controversies: Vaccines.*

CHAPTER 1

Are Vaccines Effective in the Prevention of Disease?

Overview: Immunity from Disease by Vaccination

College of Physicians of Philadelphia

The College of Physicians of Philadelphia is a nonprofit organization that advances the cause of health through such projects as the History of Vaccines, an award-winning educational website.

All living things are subject to attack from disease-causing agents. Even bacteria, so small that more than a million could fit on the head of a pin, have systems to defend against infection by viruses. This kind of protection gets more sophisticated as organisms become more complex.

The Immune System

Multicellular animals have dedicated cells or tissues to deal with the threat of infection. Some of these responses happen immediately so that an infecting agent can be quickly contained. Other responses are slower but are more tailored to the infecting agent. Collectively, these protections are known as the immune system. The human immune system is essential for our survival in a world full of potentially dangerous microbes, and serious impairment of even one arm of this system can predispose to severe, even life-threatening, infections.

The human immune system has two levels of immunity: specific and non-specific immunity. Through non-specific immunity, also called innate immunity, the human body protects itself against foreign material that is perceived to be harmful. Microbes as small as viruses and bacteria can be attacked, as can larger organisms such as worms. Collectively, these organisms are called pathogens when they cause disease in the host.

All animals have innate immune defenses against common pathogens. These first lines of defense include outer barriers like the skin and mucous membranes. When pathogens breach the outer barriers, for example through a cut in the skin or when inhaled into the lungs, they can cause serious harm.

Some white blood cells (phagocytes) fight pathogens that make it past outer defenses. A phagocyte surrounds a pathogen, takes it in, and neutralizes it.

In contrast to innate immunity, specific immunity allows for a targeted response against a specific pathogen.

Specific Immunity

While healthy phagocytes are critical to good health, they are unable to address certain infectious threats. Specific immunity is a complement to the function of phagocytes and other elements of the innate immune system.

In contrast to innate immunity, specific immunity allows for a targeted response against a specific pathogen. Only vertebrates have specific immune responses.

Two types of white blood cells called lymphocytes are vital to the specific immune response. Lymphocytes are produced in the bone marrow, and mature into one of several subtypes. The two most common are T cells and B cells.

An antigen is a foreign material that triggers a response from T and B cells. The human body has B and T cells specific to millions of different antigens. We usually think of antigens as part of microbes, but antigens can be present in other settings. For example, if a person received a blood transfusion that did not match his blood type, it could trigger reactions from T and B cells.

T Cells and B Cells

A useful way to think of T cells and B cells is as follows: B cells have one property that is essential. They can mature and differentiate into plasma cells that produce a protein called an antibody. This protein is specifically targeted to a particular antigen. However, B cells alone are not very good at making antibody and rely on T cells to provide a signal that they should begin the process of maturation. When a properly informed B cell recognizes the antigen it is coded to respond to, it divides and produces many plasma cells. The plasma cells then secrete large numbers of antibodies, which are proteins that fight specific antigens circulating in the blood.

Vaccination works to stimulate a specific immune response that will create B and T cell responses specific to a certain pathogen.

T cells are activated when a particular phagocyte known as an antigen-presenting cell (APC) displays the antigen to which the T cell is specific. This blended cell (mostly human but displaying an antigen to the T cell) is a trigger for the various elements of the specific immune response.

A subtype of T cell known as a T helper cell performs a number of roles. T helper cells release chemicals to

- Help activate B cells to divide into plasma cells when a threat has been contained and then send out signals to stop the attack.

The cells that make up the specific immune response circulate in the blood, but they are also found in a variety of organs. Within the organ, immune tissues allow for maturation of immune cells, trap pathogens and provide a place where immune cells can interact with one another and mount a specific response. Organs and tissues involved in the immune system include the thymus, bone marrow, lymph nodes, spleen, appendix, tonsils, and Peyer's patches (in the small intestine).

Infection and Disease

Infection occurs when a pathogen invades body cells and re-produces. Infection will usually lead to an immune response. If the response is quick and effective, the infection will be eliminated or contained so quickly that the disease will not occur.

Sometimes infection leads to disease. (Here we will focus on infectious disease, and define it as a state of infection that is marked by symptoms or evidence of illness.) Disease can occur when immunity is low or impaired, when virulence of the pathogen (its ability to damage host cells) is high, and when the number of pathogens in the body is great.

Depending on the infectious disease, symptoms can vary greatly. Fever is a common response to infection: a higher body temperature can heighten the immune response and provide a hostile environment for pathogens. Inflammation, or swelling caused by an increase in fluid in the infected area, is a sign that white blood cells are on the attack and releasing substances involved in the immune response.

Vaccination works to stimulate a specific immune response that will create B and T cell responses specific to a certain pathogen. After vaccination or natural infection, long-lasting memory cells persist in the body and can lead to a quick and effective response should the body encounter the pathogen again.

Vaccines Are Effective in Preventing Many Diseases

National Institute of Allergy and Infectious Diseases

The National Institute of Allergy and Infectious Diseases, a part of the National Institutes of Health within the US Department of Heath and Human Services, conducts research to better prevent infectious, immunologic, and allergic diseases.

Chances are you never had diphtheria. You probably don't know anyone who has suffered from this disease, either. In fact, you may not know what diphtheria is, exactly. Similarly, diseases like whooping cough (pertussis), measles, mumps, and German measles (rubella) may be unfamiliar to you. In the 19th and early 20th centuries, these illnesses struck hundreds of thousands of people in the United States each year, mostly children, and tens of thousands of people died. The names of these diseases were frightening household words. Today, they are all but forgotten. That change happened largely because of vaccines.

Vaccines and the Immune System

Chances are you've been vaccinated against diphtheria. You even may have been exposed to the bacterium that causes it, but the vaccine prepared your body to fight off the disease so quickly that you were unaware of the infection.

Vaccines take advantage of your body's natural ability to learn how to eliminate almost any disease-causing germ, or microbe, that attacks it. What's more, your body "remembers" how to protect itself from the microbes it has encountered before. Collectively, the parts of your body that recall and repel microbes are called the immune system. Without the immune

National Institute of Allergy and Infectious Diseases, "What Is a Vaccine? Understanding Vaccines: What They Are, How They Work," National Institutes of Health, US Department of Health and Human Services, January 2008, pp. 2–9.

system, the simplest illness—even the common cold—could quickly turn deadly. On average, your immune system takes more than a week to learn how to fight off an unfamiliar microbe. Sometimes that isn't soon enough. Stronger microbes can spread through your body faster than the immune system can fend them off. Your body often gains the upper hand after a few weeks, but in the meantime you are sick. Certain microbes are so powerful, or virulent, that they can overwhelm or escape your body's natural defenses. In those situations, vaccines can make all the difference.

Traditional vaccines contain either parts of microbes or whole microbes that have been killed or weakened so that they don't cause disease. When your immune system confronts these harmless versions of the germs, it quickly clears them from your body. In other words, vaccines trick your immune system but at the same time teach your body important lessons about how to defeat its opponents.

Before vaccines, the only way to become immune to a disease was to actually get it and, with luck, survive it.

The Benefits of Vaccines

Once your immune system is trained to resist a disease, you are said to be immune to it. Before vaccines, the only way to become immune to a disease was to actually get it and, with luck, survive it. This is called naturally acquired immunity. With naturally acquired immunity, you suffer the symptoms of the disease and also risk the complications, which can be quite serious or even deadly. In addition, during certain stages of the illness, you may be contagious and pass the disease to family members, friends, or others who come into contact with you.

Vaccines, which provide artificially acquired immunity, are an easier and less risky way to become immune. Vaccines can prevent a disease from occurring in the first place, rather than attempt a cure after the fact. It is much cheaper to prevent a disease than to treat it. According to one U.S. analysis, for every dollar spent on the measles/mumps/rubella vaccine, 21 dollars are saved.

Vaccines protect not only yourself but also others around you. If your vaccine-primed immune system stops an illness before it starts, you will be contagious for a much shorter period of time, or perhaps not at all. Similarly, when other people are vaccinated, they are less likely to give the disease to you. So vaccines protect not only individuals, but entire communities. That is why vaccines are vital to the public health goal of preventing diseases.

Herd Immunity

If a critical number of people within a community are vaccinated against a particular illness, the entire group becomes less likely to get the disease. This protection is called community immunity, or herd immunity.

On the other hand, if too many people in a community do not get vaccinations, diseases can reappear. In 1974, the Japanese government stopped vaccinating against pertussis because of public concern about the vaccine's safety and because no one had died from the disease the previous year. Five years later, a pertussis epidemic in Japan sickened 13,000 people and killed 41.

In 1989, low vaccination rates allowed a measles outbreak to occur in the United States. The outbreak resulted in more than 55,000 cases of measles and 136 measles-associated deaths.

Vaccines protect against infectious diseases caused by microbes—organisms too small to see without a microscope. Many microbes, such as bacteria, are made up of only one cell. Viruses, mere snippets of genetic material packed inside a membrane or a protein shell, are even smaller.

Humans evolved an immune system because the world is teeming with these organisms. Many of them don't bother us; the bacteria that normally live in your digestive tract are, in fact, beneficial. But other microbes break into and take up residence in your body, using your warmth, nutrients, and tissues to survive and reproduce—and doing you great harm in the process.

Diseases Prevented by Vaccines

A few examples of the most serious disease-causing microbes for which vaccines have proved highly effective include the following.

Variola virus, which causes smallpox, was once the scourge of the world. This virus passes from person to person through the air. A smallpox infection results in fever, severe aches and pains, scarring sores that cover the body, blindness in many cases, and, often, death. In the 18th century, variola virus killed every 7th child born in Russia and every 10th child born in Sweden and France.

The last case of naturally occurring smallpox was in Somalia in 1977.

Although vaccination and outbreak control had eliminated smallpox in the United States by 1949, the disease still struck an estimated 50 million people worldwide each year during the 1950s. In 1967, that figure fell to 10 to 15 million because of vaccination. That same year, the World Health Organization (WHO) launched a massive vaccination campaign to rid the world of smallpox—and succeeded. The last case of naturally occurring smallpox was in Somalia in 1977.

The highly infectious poliovirus, the cause of polio, once crippled 13,000 to 20,000 people every year in the United States. In 1954, the year before the first polio vaccine was introduced, doctors reported more than 18,000 cases of paralyzing polio in the United States. Just 3 years later, vaccination brought that figure down to about 2,500. Today, the disease has been eliminated from the Western Hemisphere, and public health officials hope to soon eradicate it from the globe. In 2006, 2,000 cases of polio were reported worldwide, according to WHO.

The Success of Vaccines

The toxic bacterium *Bordetella pertussis* likes to set up home in the human respiratory tract, where it causes whooping cough, also known as pertussis. The wracking coughs characteristic of this disease are sometimes so intense, the victims, usually infants, vomit or turn blue from lack of air. Before scientists created a vaccine against the bacterium, 115,000 to 270,000 people suffered from whooping cough each year in the United States; 5,000 to 10,000 of those died from it. After the vaccine was introduced in the United States in the 1940s, the number of pertussis cases declined dramatically, hitting a low of about 1,000 in 1976. More recently, the annual number of reported cases of pertussis in the United States has been rising from 9,771 in 2002 to 25,616 in 2005. The reasons for the increase are complex. The disease strikes in cycles, and the immunity provided by the vaccine wanes over time, leaving some people susceptible in their teen years and as adults.

Other familiar diseases that vaccines protect against include chickenpox, hepatitis A, hepatitis B, and *Haemophilus influenzae* type b *(Hib)*. Hib causes meningitis, an inflammation of the fluid-filled membranes that surround the brain and spinal cord. Meningitis can be fatal, or it can cause severe disabilities such as deafness or mental retardation. This disease has nearly disappeared among babies and children in the United States since the Hib vaccine became widely used in 1989.

Newer vaccines include one to prevent the painful condition called shingles, which can strike anyone who has ever had chickenpox; a vaccine against human papillomavirus, which can cause cervical cancer; and a vaccine against rotavirus, which causes severe diarrheal disease and some 600,000 deaths in children worldwide every year.

Many Deadly Diseases Would Return If We Stopped Vaccinations

Centers for Disease Control and Prevention (CDC)

The Centers for Disease Control and Prevention works to protect health and promote quality of life through the prevention and control of disease, injury, and disability.

In the U.S., vaccines have reduced or eliminated many infectious diseases that once routinely killed or harmed many infants, children, and adults. However, the viruses and bacteria that cause vaccine-preventable disease and death still exist and can be passed on to people who are not protected by vaccines. Vaccine-preventable diseases have many social and economic costs: sick children miss school and can cause parents to lose time from work. These diseases also result in doctor's visits, hospitalizations, and even premature deaths.

The Polio Vaccine

Stopping vaccination against polio will leave people susceptible to infection with the polio virus. Polio virus causes acute paralysis that can lead to permanent physical disability and even death. Before polio vaccine was available, 13,000 to 20,000 cases of paralytic polio were reported each year in the United States. These annual epidemics of polio often left thousands of victims—mostly children—in braces, crutches, wheelchairs, and iron lungs. The effects were life-long.

In 1988 the World Health Assembly unanimously agreed to eradicate polio worldwide. As a result of global polio eradication efforts, the number of cases reported globally has de-

Centers for Disease Control and Prevention (CDC), "What Would Happen If We Stopped Vaccinations?" US Department of Health and Human Services, August 27, 2010.

creased from more than 350,000 cases in 125 countries in 1988 to 2,000 cases of polio in 17 countries in 2006, and only four countries remain endemic (Afghanistan, India, Nigeria, Pakistan). To date polio has been eliminated from the Western hemisphere, and the European and Western Pacific regions. Stopping vaccination before eradication is achieved would result in a resurgence of the disease in the United States and worldwide.

Stopping vaccination against polio will leave people susceptible to infection with the polio virus.

The Measles Vaccine

Before measles immunization was available, nearly everyone in the U.S. got measles. An average of 450 measles-associated deaths were reported each year between 1953 and 1963.

In the U.S., *up to 20 percent of persons with measles are hospitalized.* Seventeen percent of measles cases have had one or more complications, such as ear infections, pneumonia, or diarrhea. Pneumonia is present in about six percent of cases and accounts for most of the measles deaths. Although less common, some persons with measles develop encephalitis (swelling of the lining of the brain), resulting in brain damage.

As many as three of every 1,000 persons with measles will die in the U.S. In the developing world, the rate is much higher, with death occurring in about one of every 100 persons with measles.

Measles is one of the most infectious diseases in the world and is frequently imported into the U.S. In the period 1997–2000, most cases were associated with international visitors or U.S. residents who were exposed to the measles virus while traveling abroad. More than 90 percent of people who are not immune will get measles if they are exposed to the virus.

According to the World Health Organization (WHO), nearly 900,000 measles-related deaths occurred among persons in developing countries in 1999. In populations that are not immune to measles, measles spreads rapidly. *If vaccinations were stopped, each year about 2.7 million measles deaths worldwide could be expected.*

In the U.S., widespread use of measles vaccine has led to a greater than 99 percent reduction in measles compared with the pre-vaccine era. If we stopped immunization, measles would increase to pre-vaccine levels.

The Hib Meningitis Vaccine

Before Hib vaccine became available, Hib was the most common cause of bacterial meningitis in U.S. infants and children. Before the vaccine was developed, there were approximately 20,000 invasive Hib cases annually. Approximately two-thirds of the 20,000 cases were meningitis, and one-third were other life-threatening invasive Hib diseases such as bacteria in the blood, pneumonia, or inflammation of the epiglottis. About one of every 200 U.S. children under 5 years of age got an invasive Hib disease. *Hib meningitis once killed 600 children each year and left many survivors with deafness, seizures, or mental retardation.*

Since introduction of conjugate Hib vaccine in December 1987, the incidence of Hib has declined by 98 percent. From 1994–1998, fewer than 10 fatal cases of invasive Hib disease were reported each year.

This preventable disease was a common, devastating illness as recently as 1990; now, most pediatricians just finishing training have never seen a case. If we were to stop immunization, we would likely soon return to the pre-vaccine numbers of invasive Hib disease cases and deaths.

The Pertussis Vaccine

Since the early 1980s, reported pertussis cases have been increasing, with peaks every 3–5 years; however, the number of reported cases remains much lower than levels seen in the pre-vaccine era. Compared with pertussis cases in other age groups, infants who are 6 months old or younger with pertussis experience the highest rate of hospitalization, pneumonia, seizures, encephalopathy (a degenerative disease of the brain) and death. From 2000 through 2008, 181 persons died from pertussis; 166 of these were less than six months old.

Before Hib vaccine became available, Hib was the most common cause of bacterial meningitis in U.S. infants and children.

Before pertussis immunizations were available, nearly all children developed whooping cough. In the U.S., prior to pertussis immunization, between 150,000 and 260,000 cases of pertussis were reported each year, with up to 9,000 pertussis-related deaths.

Pertussis can be a severe illness, resulting in prolonged coughing spells that can last for many weeks. These spells can make it difficult for a person to eat, drink, and breathe. Because vomiting often occurs after a coughing spell, persons may lose weight and become dehydrated. In infants, *it can also cause pneumonia and lead to brain damage, seizures, and mental retardation.*

The newer pertussis vaccine (acellular or DTaP) has been available for use in the United States since 1991 and has been recommended for exclusive use since 1998. These vaccines are effective and associated with fewer mild and moderate adverse reactions when compared with the older (whole-cell DTP) vaccines.

During the 1970s, widespread concerns about the safety of the older pertussis vaccine led to a rapid fall in immunization levels in the United Kingdom. More than 100,000 cases and 36 deaths due to pertussis were reported during an epidemic in the mid 1970s. In Japan, pertussis vaccination coverage fell from 80 percent in 1974 to 20 percent in 1979. An epidemic occurred in 1979 [and] resulted in more than 13,000 cases and 41 deaths.

Pertussis cases occur throughout the world. If we stopped pertussis immunizations in the U.S., we would experience a massive resurgence of pertussis disease. *A study found that, in eight countries where immunization coverage was reduced, incidence rates of pertussis surged to 10 to 100 times the rates in countries where vaccination rates were sustained.*

If we were to stop immunization, we would likely soon return to the pre-vaccine numbers of invasive pneumococcal disease cases and deaths.

The Pneumococcal Vaccine

Before pneumococcal conjugate vaccine became available for children, pneumococcus caused 63,000 cases of invasive pneumococcal disease and 6,100 deaths in the U.S. each year. Many children who developed pneumococcal meningitis also developed long-term complications such as deafness or seizures. Since the vaccine was introduced, the incidence of invasive pneumococcal disease in children has been reduced by 75%. Pneumococcal conjugate vaccine also reduces spread of pneumococcus from children to adults. In 2003 alone, there were 30,000 fewer cases of invasive pneumococcal disease caused by strains included in the vaccine, including 20,000 fewer cases in children and adults too old to receive the vaccine. If we were to stop immunization, we would likely soon return to the pre-vaccine numbers of invasive pneumococcal disease cases and deaths.

The Rubella Vaccine

While rubella is usually mild in children and adults, up to 90 percent of infants born to mothers infected with rubella during the first trimester of pregnancy will develop *congenital rubella syndrome (CRS), resulting in heart defects, cataracts, mental retardation, and deafness.*

In 1964–1965, before rubella immunization was used routinely in the U.S., there was an epidemic of rubella that resulted in an estimated 20,000 infants born with CRS, with 2,100 neonatal deaths and 11,250 miscarriages. Of the 20,000 infants born with CRS, 11,600 were deaf, 3,580 were blind, and 1,800 were mentally retarded.

Due to the widespread use of rubella vaccine, only six CRS cases were provisionally reported in the U.S. in 2000. Because many developing countries do not include rubella in the childhood immunization schedule, many of these cases occurred in foreign-born adults. Since 1996, greater than 50 percent of the reported rubella cases have been among adults. Since 1999, there have been 40 pregnant women infected with rubella.

If we stopped rubella immunization, immunity to rubella would decline and rubella would once again return, resulting in pregnant women becoming infected with rubella and then giving birth to infants with CRS.

The Chickenpox Vaccine

Prior to the licensing of the chickenpox vaccine in 1995, almost all persons in the United States had suffered from chickenpox by adulthood. Each year, the virus caused an estimated 4 million cases of chickenpox, 11,000 hospitalizations, and 100–150 deaths.

A highly contagious disease, chickenpox is usually mild but can be severe in some persons. Infants, adolescents and adults, pregnant women, and immunocompromised persons are at particular risk for serious complications including secondary bacterial infections, loss of fluids (dehydration), pneumonia, and central nervous system involvement. The availability of the chickenpox vaccine and its subsequent widespread use has had a major impact on reducing cases of chickenpox and related morbidity, hospitalizations, and deaths. In some areas, cases have decreased as much as 90% over prevaccination numbers.

In 2006, routine two-dose vaccination against chickenpox was recommended for all children, adolescents, and adults who do not have evidence of immunity to the disease. In addition to further reducing cases, this strategy will also decrease the risk for exposure to the virus for persons who are unable to be vaccinated because of illness or other conditions and who may develop severe disease. If vaccination against chickenpox were to stop, the disease would eventually return to prevaccination rates, with virtually all susceptible persons becoming infected with the virus at some point in their lives.

The Hepatitis B Vaccine

More than 2 billion persons worldwide have been infected with the hepatitis B virus at some time in their lives. Of these, 350 million are life-long carriers of the disease and can transmit the virus to others. *One million of these people die each year from liver disease and liver cancer.*

National studies have shown that about 12.5 million Americans have been infected with hepatitis B virus at some point in their lifetime. One and one quarter million Americans are estimated to have chronic (long-lasting) infection, of whom 20 percent to 30 percent acquired their infection in childhood. Chronic hepatitis B virus infection increases a person's risk for chronic liver disease, cirrhosis, and liver cancer. About 5,000 persons will die each year from hepatitis B-related liver disease resulting in over $700 million in medical and work loss costs.

The number of new infections per year has declined from an average of 450,000 in the 1980s to about 80,000 in 1999. The greatest decline has occurred among children and adolescents due to routine hepatitis B vaccination.

Infants and children who become infected with hepatitis B virus are at highest risk of developing lifelong infection, which often leads to death from liver disease (cirrhosis) and liver cancer. *Approximately 25 percent of children who become infected with life-long hepatitis B virus would be expected to die of related liver disease as adults.*

CDC [Centers for Disease Control and Prevention] estimates that one-third of the life-long hepatitis B virus infections in the United States resulted from infections occurring in infants and young children. About 16,000–20,000 hepatitis B antigen infected women give birth each year in the United States. It is estimated that 12,000 children born to hepatitis B virus infected mothers were infected each year before implementation of infant immunization programs. In addition, approximately 33,000 children (10 years of age and younger) of mothers who are not infected with hepatitis B virus were infected each year before routine recommendation of childhood hepatitis B vaccination.

In the 1920's, diphtheria was a major cause of illness and death for children in the U.S.

The Diphtheria Vaccine

Diphtheria is a serious disease caused by a bacterium. This germ produces a poisonous substance or toxin which frequently causes heart and nerve problems. The case fatality rate is 5 percent to 10 percent, with higher case-fatality rates (up to 20 percent) in the very young and the elderly.

In the 1920's, diphtheria was a major cause of illness and death for children in the U.S. In 1921, a total of 206,000 cases and 15,520 deaths were reported. With vaccine development in 1923, new cases of diphtheria began to fall in the U.S., until in 2001 only two cases were reported.

Although diphtheria is rare in the U.S., it appears that the bacteria continue to get passed among people. In 1996, 10 isolates of the bacteria were obtained from persons in an American Indian community in South Dakota, none of whom had classic diphtheria disease. There was one death reported in 2003 from clinical diphtheria in a 63 year old male who had never been vaccinated.

There are high rates of susceptibility among adults. Screening tests conducted since 1977 have shown that 41 percent to 84 percent of adults 60 and over lack protective levels of circulating antitoxin against diphtheria.

Although diphtheria is rare in the U.S., it is still a threat. Diphtheria is common in other parts of the world and with the increase in international travel, *diphtheria and other infectious diseases are only a plane ride away*. If we stopped immunization, the U.S. might experience a situation similar to the Newly Independent States of the former Soviet Union. With the breakdown of the public health services in this area, diphtheria epidemics began in 1990, fueled primarily by persons who were not properly vaccinated. From 1990–1999, more than 150,000 cases and 5,000 deaths were reported.

The Tetanus Vaccine

Tetanus is a severe, often fatal disease. The bacteria that cause tetanus are widely distributed in soil and street dust, are found in the waste of many animals, and are very resistant to heat and germ-killing cleaners. From 1922–1926, there were an estimated 1,314 cases of tetanus per year in the U.S. In the late 1940's, the tetanus vaccine was introduced, and tetanus became a disease that was officially counted and tracked by public health officials. In 2000, only 41 cases of tetanus were reported in the U.S.

People who get tetanus suffer from stiffness and spasms of the muscles. The larynx (throat) can close causing breathing and eating difficulties, muscles spasms can cause fractures (breaks) of the spine and long bones, and some people go into a coma, and die. *Approximately 20 percent of reported cases end in death.*

Tetanus in the U.S. is primarily a disease of adults, but unvaccinated children and infants of unvaccinated mothers are also at risk for tetanus and neonatal tetanus, respectively. From 1995–1997, 33 percent of reported cases of tetanus occurred among persons 60 years of age or older and 60 percent occurred in patients greater than 40 years of age. The National Health Interview Survey found that in 1995, only 36 percent of adults 65 or older had received a tetanus vaccination during the preceding 10 years.

Worldwide, tetanus in newborn infants continues to be a huge problem. Every year *tetanus kills 300,000 newborns and 30,000 birth mothers who were not properly vaccinated.* Even though the number of reported cases is low, an increased number of tetanus cases in younger persons has been observed recently in the U.S. among intravenous drug users, particularly heroin users.

Before there was a vaccine against mumps, mumps was a very common disease in U.S. children, with as many as 300,000 cases reported every year.

Tetanus is infectious, but not contagious, so unlike other vaccine-preventable diseases, immunization by members of the community will not protect others from the disease. Because tetanus bacteria are widespread in the environment, tetanus can only be prevented by immunization. If vaccination against tetanus were stopped, persons of all ages in the U.S. would be susceptible to this serious disease.

The Mumps Vaccine

Before the mumps vaccine was introduced, mumps was a major cause of deafness in children, occurring in approximately 1 in

20,000 reported cases. Mumps is usually a mild viral disease. However, serious complications, such as inflammation of the brain (encephalitis) can occur rarely. Prior to mumps vaccine, mumps encephalitis was the leading cause of viral encephalitis in the United States, but is now rarely seen.

Serious side effects of mumps are more common among adults than children. Swelling of the testes is the most common side effect in males past the age of puberty, occurring in up to 37 percent of post-pubertal males who contract mumps. *An increase in miscarriages has been found among women who develop mumps during the first trimester of pregnancy.*

Before there was a vaccine against mumps, mumps was a very common disease in U.S. children, with as many as 300,000 cases reported every year. After vaccine licensure in 1967, reports of mumps decreased rapidly. In 1986 and 1987, there was a resurgence of mumps with 12,848 cases reported in 1987. Since 1989, the incidence of mumps has declined, with 266 reported cases in 2001. This recent decrease is probably due to the fact that children have received a second dose of mumps vaccine (part of the two-dose schedule for measles, mumps, rubella or MMR). Studies have shown that the effectiveness of mumps vaccine ranges from 73% to 91% after 1 dose and from 79% to 95% after 2 doses and that 2 doses are more effective than 1 dose.

We can not let our guard down against mumps. A 2006 outbreak among college students led to over 6,500 cases and a 2009–10 outbreak in the tradition-observant Jewish community in 2 states led to over 3,400 cases. Mumps is a communicable disease and while prolonged close contact among persons may facilitate transmission, maintenance of high 2-dose MMR vaccine coverage remains the most effective way to prevent and limit the size of mumps outbreaks.

There Is Evidence That Vaccines Promote, Rather than Eradicate, Disease

Alex Newman

Alex Newman is a freelance writer and the president of Liberty Sentinel Media, Inc., a media consulting firm located in Gainesville, Florida.

Death from the flu is often heartrending for those who have to watch: the victim, having been weakened from the flu virus, contracts pneumonia from bacteria or viruses that have taken hold in the lungs, and he or she struggles for every breath.

The victim's breathing is often raspy, and it is abnormally fast, like the panting of a worn-out dog. As the victim's body fights the lung infection, the lungs fill with pus and other fluids, cutting off the flow of oxygen and causing the victim to turn colors—from shades of gray to a bluish purple. The victim's struggle to breathe can last for hours and hours.

The Flu

Between 30,000 to 40,000 people die of the flu each year according to the Centers for Disease Control (CDC), so it's understandable that Americans are willing to line up in doctors' offices, and even in grocery stores, to get flu shots to ward off the possibility of catching the flu—especially with the dreaded swine flu prevalent this year [2009]. (In 1918–1919, the Spanish flu, an ancestor of the modern swine flu, reportedly killed upwards of 50 million people worldwide.)

Government entities are taking seriously the threat of a repeat of the morbidity and death rates of the 1918–1919 flu.

The United Nations recently claimed millions around the world would die if rich countries refused to provide billions of dollars for vaccines. In the United States, the President's Council of Advisors on Science and Technology recently issued a dire warning entitled "On US Preparations for 2009-H1N1 Influenza" about the potential spread of the virus later on this year. It claimed that a "plausible scenario" would be "infection of 30–50 percent of the U.S. population this fall and winter, with symptoms in approximately 20–40 percent of the population (60–120 million people), more than half of whom would seek medical attention."

While acknowledging that the true impact is impossible to predict, the report said the H1N1 virus could result in up to 1.8 million hospital admissions with as many as 300,000 people requiring hospitalization in intensive care units [the CDC estimates there were between 195,000 and 403,000 hospitalizations]. This would place "enormous stress" on intensive care units, with between 50 to 100 percent of beds occupied.

"It's a plausible scenario that we need to be prepared for," said Marty Cetron, the CDC's director of the Division of Global Migration and Quarantine.

A growing chorus of doctors and researchers is claiming that being injected with the swine flu vaccine may be more hazardous than catching the flu.

The answer to the swine flu, according to most public officials, is a worldwide flu vaccination campaign. The United States is on board. The coming swine flu vaccination campaign will be the first time the U.S. government has ever attempted to vaccinate so many people in such a short time frame.

But even as governments around the world create vaccines and run TV and radio ads convincing the public to get vaccinated (Health and Human Services Secretary Kathleen Sebelius even promoted the vaccine for the seasonal flu and the swine flu on NBC's *Today* show), and people prepare to line up to get their shots and boost their immunity, a growing chorus of doctors and researchers is claiming that being injected with the swine flu vaccine may be more hazardous than catching the flu. . . .

The Safety of the Flu Vaccine

Even though this strain of the swine flu is appearing quite mild, the creation and testing of the vaccine is taking place at a rate that calls into question the safety of the flu shot. Sharon Frey, who is leading the government vaccine testing at St. Louis University, told the Associated Press, "Typically it takes a year to do this," adding, "We're working at breakneck speed."

To cut time, corners are likely being cut: inoculations may start before the speedy trials are even over, according to the head of the flu vaccination program at the CDC. Safety tests are being fast-tracked under "public health emergency" rules.

Even if the vaccines were being developed in a safe manner, with safe ingredients, vaccines are not necessarily going to protect someone from getting a certain virus.

This fast-tracking is happening worldwide. Dr. Marc Girard, a specialist in medicine who is commissioned by the French courts, told France 24 in a televised interview that the vaccine could very well cause 60,000 deaths in France alone. "We are developing a vaccine under conditions of amateurism that I have never seen before," he said, noting that the nation's immunization program was placing the public health in grave danger. He added that the government has a duty to protect citizens from the corrupt companies pushing their vaccines, and that people who are creating hysteria about the swine flu or promoting the vaccine have other interests. The channel's health expert agreed with him, warning of the elevated mercury levels and other toxins in the vaccine.

A lack of testing is of more than minor concern. In the United Kingdom, the government's Health Protection Agency (HPA) sent a letter to senior neurologists warning that the new swine flu vaccine is linked to the deadly nerve disease known as Guillain-Barre Syndrome (GBS), the *Daily Mail* reported in an article entitled "Swine flu jab link to killer nerve disease." The leaked HPA letter warned recipients to keep an eye open for GBS and report it immediately.

During the swine flu scare of 1976 in the United States, the risk of contracting the paralysis-inducing illness was reportedly eight times greater in those who received the infamous government swine flu vaccine of that year, compared to those who did not. And the shot killed far more people than the actual virus. . . .

The Effectiveness of Vaccines

Even if the vaccines were being developed in a safe manner, with safe ingredients, vaccines are not necessarily going to protect someone from getting a certain virus. If the disease mutates, as must happen if the swine flu is to become a major health threat, the inoculation will likely be essentially useless because human antibodies are generally virus-specific. But even if the virus were not to mutate, and even if it were extremely lethal (which it is not), the vaccine may not offer protection.

"So-called pandemic vaccines, well we never know whether they'll work," explained Tom Jefferson, an epidemiologist at the Cochrane Institute, about what he believed was an unjustified panic regarding the swine flu. "What the evidence shows, from the hundreds of studies that we have reviewed, is that these vaccines have got a performance [record] which is not very good." He told a Swedish television station that the immunizations usually work best in healthy adults, who are the lowest priority for receiving them anyway, and that the reason for the hysteria is the interests of those selling "a product."

Dr. Sherri Tenpenny, one of the leading experts on the dangers of vaccines, shows in various presentations—using statistics and data gathered from the CDC and other official sources—that vaccines' efficacy leaves much to be desired, yet they expose recipients to a wide array of risks. She notes that the immunizations given to children usually only last a number of years, and that "the presence of antibodies does not guarantee that you will not get sick." The potential immunity obtained from a hepatitis vaccine, for example, is gone in a majority of people within around 10 years. This is the reason people are often re-vaccinated. According to Dr. Tenpenny, most antibodies babies get are "all gone" by the time they are 12 years old. She continued by explaining: "If they inject you with a substance and it creates an antibody, they call it effective. It is one of the biggest myths—maybe scams—of the entire vaccine industry." Verifying part of her claim, the WHO [World Health Organization] is already warning that the virus is developing resistance to the vaccine. So even the presence of an immune response does not mean it will offer protection.

A Counterintuitive Effect

Vaccines are not safe and effective, Dr. Tenpenny insists. They are linked to problems like allergies, diabetes, and a host of medical problems. For example, research and published studies by immunologist and president of Classen Immunotherapies Dr. Bart Classen have shown that vaccines cause up to 80 percent of insulin-dependent diabetes in children vaccinated multiple times. In addition, vaccines are not responsible for the elimination of infectious diseases. They may in fact be causing a resurgence of the diseases that they purport to protect against. "I really think that it is the greatest deception ever propagated on an unsuspecting public—that doing something in the name of health and helping is in fact plausibly detrimental and potentially life threatening."

Counterintuitively, the facts seem to back her up. A CDC chart on the efficacy of seasonal vaccines shows that flu deaths were steadily decreasing until vaccine programs were rolled out, then flu cases burgeoned. For example, in 1980, about 20 percent of the elderly population was covered by immunizations, and there were about 20 deaths per 100,000 elderly people. Then in the year 2000, when approximately 65 percent of the elderly population had vaccine coverage, deaths had soared to almost 35 per 100,000. The trend is consistent and immediately obvious even to the untrained eye.

Many medical experts agree that, in addition to outright catastrophes that are attributed to vaccines, history shows that the benefits of vaccines are dubious at best.

"Most people believe that victory over the infectious diseases of the last century came with the invention of immunisations," writes Dr. Andrew Weil in *Health and Healing*. "In fact, cholera, typhoid, tetanus, diphtheria and whooping cough, etc., were in decline before vaccines for them became available—the result of better methods of sanitation, sewage disposal, and distribution of food and water."

Criticism of Vaccination

Many medical experts agree that, in addition to outright catastrophes that are attributed to vaccines, history shows that the benefits of vaccines are dubious at best.

Criticism of government vaccination programs is nothing new. "The greatest threat of childhood diseases lies in the dangerous and ineffectual efforts made to prevent them through mass immunization," noted Dr. Robert Mendelsohn in 1973. "There is no convincing scientific evidence that mass inoculations can be credited with eliminating any childhood disease." His damning analysis of vaccines applies across the board.

The most relevant and frequently cited example in relation to the current program is the mass immunization program of 1976 against a supposed outbreak of the swine flu virus. The only people to vote against the program in the House of Representatives were Congressmen Ron Paul and Larry McDonald, both medical doctors. Not only was their vote the only constitutionally appropriate one, the decision to implement the program later proved to be an absolute disaster. "Medically it made no sense to me and politically it sounded like a bad deal," Rep. Paul recalled in an interview with CNN last May [2009]. "Dr. Larry McDonald and I said it was bad medicine, it was bad politics, and it turned out that it was pretty perceptive," he added, noting that far more people died from the vaccine than the virus.

The Swine Flu of 1976

The politicalization of the swine flu scare of 1976 followed a predictable course. After some recruits at Fort Dix in New Jersey contracted the swine flu, the Advisory Committee on Immunization Practices of the United States Public Health Service recommended that the entire U.S. population be vaccinated. The CDC and the federal government decided it was necessary to spend almost $150 million to immunize "every man, woman and child."

Following a massive government propaganda operation, more potent than the one being witnessed today, millions of Americans dutifully lined up to get their shot. It was safe, effective, and necessary, government officials assured the populace. But the government officials lied.

By the time the dust had settled, only one person's death had been linked to contracting the swine flu, while hundreds of deaths and thousands of grave neurological disorders were attributed to the vaccine. The campaign was suspended after just 10 weeks as the reports of side effects—often fatal—continued to pour in from around the country.

The "pandemic" never materialized, but since the government had agreed to exempt vaccine manufacturers from liability (much like today), taxpayers were on the hook for billions in damages. One of the most common horrors and widely reported consequences of the immunization was the emergence of the paralyzing neurological disease Guillain-Barre Syndrome in some inoculated Americans. Documents prove the CDC knew about the potential for these effects, but citizens were never informed. A CBS *60 Minutes* investigation also revealed that the government had even lied in claims it made saying that certain well-known figures had taken the vaccine.

Questionable Immunization Schemes

In addition to the 1976 "fiasco," as it was dubbed, a wide variety of other government vaccination debacles have been highlighted by medical experts and opponents of the swine flu vaccine—such as the outbreak of smallpox in the 1920s. Dr. True Ott wrote in a widely publicized article entitled "Vaccine-induced Disease Epidemic Outbreaks" that the spread of smallpox was actually caused by the government vaccine, which used live viruses.

"The Protective Bureau proved in court that there was no epidemic before the vaccinations," he said, referring to the watchdog group Advertiser's Protective Bureau in Kansas City, Missouri, and the smallpox epidemic in the early twenties. "The court record on this case is very clear. In the weeks and months following the 'mass vaccinations' the area's hospital beds were filled to over-flowing with vaccine-induced smallpox cases."

Ian Sinclair, an author and vaccination researcher who has studied the issues for over 20 years, points to a slew of other cases of immunization schemes that in retrospect turned out to be disastrous. He provides compelling historical examples from a variety of sources including governments and medical journals, noting that he believes vaccines are "biological poisons" that offer no protection whatsoever and are actually a contributing factor in disease.

When the German government rolled out its compulsory immunization against diphtheria in 1940, there were 40,000 reported deaths from the illness, Sinclair notes. In 1945, 250,000 people died from the disease. Sweden stopped its whooping cough vaccination program in 1979 when it was discovered that 84 percent of the children who fell ill from the disease had been vaccinated against it three times. And a study published in 1994 in the *New England Journal of Medicine* noted that more than 80 percent of American children under five with whooping cough had been fully vaccinated.

In addition to the 1976 "fiasco," as it was dubbed, a wide variety of other government vaccination debacles have been highlighted by medical experts.

A 1970s vaccine study in India revealed that tuberculosis occurred more often in people who had taken the shot than in those who had not. In the United Kingdom, Sinclair points out, the Community Disease Surveillance Center acknowledges over 200,000 cases of whooping cough in fully vaccinated children between 1970 and 1990. An outbreak of polio in Oman in the late 1980s struck hardest in areas where vaccination was widespread. The polio vaccine has also been implicated in the spread of a virus known as SV 40 as a result of the monkeys used in its preparation. It is linked to cancer and a host of other problems.

The WHO has also been accused of sparking the AIDS epidemic in Africa via its smallpox vaccination campaign. "I thought it was just a coincidence until we studied the latest findings about the reactions which can be caused by Vaccinia," a WHO advisor told the *London Times* in a 1987 article entitled "Smallpox vaccine 'triggered Aids virus.'" "Now I believe the smallpox vaccine theory is the explanation to the explosion of Aids." The article continued by noting that "the greatest spread of HIV infection coincides with the most intense immunization programmes."

The Eradication of Disease

The global health "authorities" have made plenty of other significant blunders and miscalculations as well. In 1967, the WHO declared that Ghana was measles-free after 96 percent of the population was vaccinated. But just five years later, the country suffered its most deadly outbreak of the disease.

While governments like to take credit for success in eradicating disease and protecting the public, this is not generally the reality.

A 1990 article about measles in the *Journal of the American Medical Association* pointed out: "Although more than 95% of school-aged children in the US are vaccinated against measles, large measles outbreaks continue to occur in schools and most cases in this setting occur among previously vaccinated children." And particularly telling, in 1977, Dr. Jonas Salk, the developer of the first polio vaccine, testified with other scientists that the cause of most polio cases in the United States since 1961 was the inoculation itself.

So while governments like to take credit for success in eradicating disease and protecting the public, this is not generally the reality. In fact, governments and their programs often cause disasters under the guise of caring for citizens, and improved health has much more to do with other factors—like capitalism, freedom, and the higher standard of living those entail—than with improved vaccines.

This is just a small sampling of the damning body of evidence mounting against the cause of vaccinations and their government sponsors. Sinclair and others have highlighted many more examples. There are massive amounts of information available about these issues, so it is certainly worth considering in light of the new swine flu program—especially with the revelations that the new vaccine has been fast-tracked through safety tests under the guise of an "emergency" and some side effects take considerable time to appear.

Vaccines Have Not Been Proven to Be Safe or Effective

Sherri Tenpenny

Sherri Tenpenny is a medical doctor who advocates for free choice in healthcare, including the right to refuse vaccination.

A chilling, consistent pattern exists in stories told by parents: My child was normal, happy, and healthy. He was walking, learning to talk and playing with his siblings. He was on track developmentally, and everything was normal. At his one-year well baby check up, the doctor said it was time for his next round of shots. Unquestioning, the shots were given. Within weeks, he was autistic.

The reports vary slightly in content and timing, but the descriptions of thousands of children who suddenly regress into the isolated world of autism are eerily the same.

Dogmas in Medicine

Webster's [dictionary] defines dogma as "a doctrine; a positive arrogant assertion of opinion." Taking off from this definition, medical dogmas certainly abound. Many have survived for decades simply because an assertion was made and then never questioned. Over time, the allegation was assumed to be fact.

An early example of dogma in the vaccine industry occurred in 1913 when Dr. Simon Flexnor held out that polio was a disease caused by a virus entering the body through the nose and mouth. He postulated that paralysis arose when the virus traveled directly from the sinuses to the brain and the spinal cord. Flexnor's assertions about the mode of paralysis were never reproduced and it is now known that polio is a gastrointestinal virus, not a respiratory virus.

Difficulties in developing a vaccine occurred because he propagated a dogma that the polio virus would only grow in neurological tissue, a culture media that was associated with life-threatening encephalitis in experimental animals. No one attempted to use other types of tissue cultures to grow polioviruses. His solo paper remained unquestioned dogma for 25 years until Dr. John Enders found, serendipitously, that the virus would indeed grow in a variety of different tissues. When Enders' revolutionary discovery was published in *Science*, January 28, 1949, the entire virology community immediately accepted the new findings. The polio vaccine was produced within five years. A scientific claim passed off as dogma vanished when challenged by scientific fact.

Present day vaccine dogma is promoted by The Institute of Medicine (IOM), a group of ostensibly impartial physicians, scientists and researchers. After reviewing the industry-funded research papers concluding there is no connection between vaccines and autism, the IOM similarly concludes there is no connection between vaccines and autism. How could they come to any other conclusion?

Present day vaccine dogma is promoted by The Institute of Medicine (IOM), a group of ostensibly impartial physicians, scientists and researchers.

Vaccines and Autism

The phrase, "temporal association does not prove causality" means that even though two events occur at the same time, one event does not cause the other. The IOM supports the dogma purported by the American Academy of Pediatrics: Since autism occurs chronologically around the same time as the first year vaccinations, angry parents need something to blame.

The medical dogma supporting this position is the assertion that "temporal association does not prove causality." Simply put, the phrase means that even though two events occur at nearly the same time, one event is not the cause of the other. The implication is that regression into autism would have happened anyway. The administration of several vaccines immediately before the appearance of autism had nothing to do with it, a dogma that promotes "the child is to blame, not the vaccine." Similarly, intense investigations are searching for a genetic cause for autism spectrum disorders. The identification of a corrupted gene will point an incriminating finger at defective parents as the "cause" of their child's autism.

The following statement was published in the Center for Disease Control's [CDC] publication on infection diseases, referred to as *The Pink Book*:

> "There is no distinct syndrome from vaccine administration, and therefore, many temporally associated adverse events probably represent background illness rather than illness caused by the vaccine. . . . The [vaccine] may stimulate or precipitate inevitable symptoms of underlying CNS [central nervous system] disorder, such as seizures, infantile spasms, epilepsy or SIDS [sudden infant death syndrome]. By chance alone, some of these cases will seem to be temporally related to [the vaccine]."

With the rate of autism being one in every 150 children in the U.S. and a new high of one in every 58 children in the U.K. [United Kingdom], an urgent investigation needs to be undertaken to establish if unvaccinated 12 to 18 month old children suddenly become autistic. There has been no answer to this question, in fact, no one has even looked.

Assumptions About Safety and Efficacy

The classic example of unquestioned dogma is the long held notion that the sun rotated around the earth. In 1530, [astronomer Nicolaus] Copernicus challenged the assumption with evidence that the earth rotated on its axis once daily and traveled around the sun once yearly. A fantastic concept for the times, the new information was considered heresy. Later, when Galileo [Galilei] supported Copernicus' conclusions, he was imprisoned, subjected to a trial by Holy Inquisitioners, and forced to withdraw his evidence to save his own life.

Similarly, parents are forced into vaccination decisions by modern day medical inquisitioners. Threats include expulsion from the medical practice and calls to children's protective services with accusations of medical neglect. Parents are told vaccines are safe and necessary for keeping children healthy. But are they really safe?

Contrary to repeated claims by the government and the pharmaceutical industry, vaccines have never been proven to be safe by the gold standard of medical research: The double-blind, placebo controlled investigation.

Vaccination is a medical treatment. Assumptions regarding the effectiveness of many medical treatments abound. A report published by The Government Accounting Office (GAO) concluded that "only 10–20% of all procedures currently used in medical practice have been shown to be efficacious by controlled trials." Hence, 80–90% of usual and customary practices are assumed to be effective without proof. Vaccination falls into this category.

Placebo-Controlled Studies

Contrary to repeated claims by the government and the pharmaceutical industry, vaccines have never been proven to be safe by the gold standard of medical research: The double-blind, placebo controlled investigation. In a placebo-controlled study, the safety of a medication is determined by comparing it to a neutral substance, such as a sugar pill. In vaccine safety trials, a new vaccine is not compared to an inert compound such as a shot of sterile water. Instead, the "placebo" is another vaccine. If the number of side effects caused by the experimental vaccine is found to be the same as the number of reactions caused by the placebo-vaccine, manufacturers declare the new vaccine to be "as safe as placebo."

Another trick used by investigators to promote the safety of vaccines is to discount any part of the study's data that suggests a problem. The following excerpt from a clinical trial demonstrates how a placebo-vaccine is used and the elimination of negative data. The study was designed to determine the safety of Comvax®, a vaccine combining the Haemophilus influenza vaccine (HiB) and the hepatitis B vaccine into one shot.

> During the study, 17 children (1.9%) had an event within 14 days of vaccination that met one of the defining criteria of a serious adverse experience. These experiences included seizure, asthma, diarrhea, apnea (stopped breathing) [and many others.] Virtually all of these adverse experiences were classified as serious because they involved a hospitalization. None was judged by the study investigators to be causally related [caused by] Comvax® or the [other two vaccines]. In addition, three deaths among participants in this study were attributed to sudden infant death syndrome that occurred more than 14 days after administration of a dose of vaccine (29, 31, and 38 days, respectively.) Again, none was judged by the investigators to be related to vaccination.

The placebo in this study was the HiB vaccine and the hepatitis b vaccine given as two separate shots. Because the number of side effects from the single shot was similar to the number of side effects induced by the separate shots, Comvax® was declared to be "as safe as placebo." Investigators nullified the association between the vaccines and SIDS with a stroke of the pen. Comvax® was declared to be "well-tolerated."

Defining Effective Vaccines

Researchers define an effective vaccine as one that creates antibodies after being deposited into the bloodstream, a response called "positive seroconversion." One vaccine is considered to be more effective than another, from a researcher's perspective, if the first vaccine induces a larger antibody response than the second.

The medical community and the general public define an effective vaccine as a vaccine that protects a person from the infection they have been vaccinated against. For example, the chickenpox vaccine is considered to be effective by doctors if, in the case of an outbreak, those vaccinated do not contract chickenpox.

The definitions differ substantially and have considerably different ramifications, mostly because the presence of an antibody does not assure the person will be protected from infection. Many outbreaks have occurred in fully vaccinated populations. One example was an outbreak of measles that occurred in a group where more than 99 percent of the population had been vaccinated. Many outbreaks of chickenpox and mumps have occurred when children were fully vaccinated.

Vaccines provide false security about protection.

The package insert of the HiBTiter®, a vaccine to protect against an infection by the H. influenza b bacteria, clearly states "the contribution [antibodies make] to clinical protection is unknown." Similar findings have been reported about the pertussis vaccine: "The findings of efficacy studies have not demonstrated a direct correlation between antibody response and protection against pertussis disease." The esteemed medical journal, *Vaccine*, states clearly, "It is known that, in many instances, antibody titers do not correlate with protection."

The Safe and Effective Dogma

The dogma that vaccines are safe and effective has become a medical sacred cow, an icon regarded to be above criticism or attack. Challenges to vaccination have often been written off as conspiracy theories. Parents have learned through experience the difficulties of challenging their pediatrician's vaccine mandates. Nonetheless, many are resisting the medical profession's dogmas about vaccines and many are refusing vaccinations for their children.

A benchmark in a civilized society is the absence of infectious diseases, a doctrine that emerged during the pre-antibiotic era. Public health officials attribute low infection rates to mandatory vaccination policies rather than giving credit to improved personal hygiene and modern conveniences such as indoor plumbing. It is time for the truth about vaccines to be widely known. Vaccine safety has not been proven. Vaccines provide false security about protection. Vaccines can cause harm. It is time to dispense with the "safe and effective" dogma before one more person is harmed.

There Is Little Evidence That Flu Vaccines Are Effective

Shannon Brownlee and Jeanne Lenzer

Shannon Brownlee is acting director of the New America Health Policy Program and author of Overtreated: Why Too Much Medicine Is Making Us Sicker and Poorer. *Jeanne Lenzer is an independent medical investigative journalist.*

Vaccination is central to the government's plan for preventing deaths from swine flu. The CDC [Centers for Disease Control and Prevention] has recommended that some 159 million adults and children receive either a swine flu shot or a dose of MedImmune's nasal vaccine this year [2009]. Shots are offered in doctors' offices, hospitals, airports, pharmacies, schools, polling places, shopping malls, and big-box stores like Wal-Mart. In August [2009], New York state required all health-care workers to get both seasonal and swine flu shots. To further protect the populace, the federal government has spent upwards of $3 billion stockpiling millions of doses of antiviral drugs like Tamiflu—which are being used both to prevent swine flu and to treat those who fall ill.

But what if everything we think we know about fighting influenza is wrong? What if flu vaccines do not protect people from dying—particularly the elderly, who account for 90 percent of deaths from seasonal flu? And what if the expensive antiviral drugs that the government has stockpiled over the past few years also have little, if any, power to reduce the number of people who die or are hospitalized? The U.S. government—with the support of leaders in the public-health and medical communities—has put its faith in the power of vaccines and antiviral drugs to limit the spread and lethality of swine flu. Other plans to contain the pandemic seem anemic by comparison. Yet some top flu researchers are deeply skeptical of both flu vaccines and antivirals. Like the engineers who warned for years about the levees of New Orleans, these experts caution that our defenses may be flawed, and quite possibly useless against a truly lethal flu. And that unless we are willing to ask fundamental questions about the science behind flu vaccines and antiviral drugs, we could find ourselves, in a bad epidemic, as helpless as the citizens of New Orleans during Hurricane Katrina [2005].

The Mysterious Nature of Flu

The term influenza, which dates back to the Middle Ages, is taken from the Italian word for occult or astral influence. Then as now, flu seemed to appear out of nowhere each winter, debilitating or killing large numbers of people, only to vanish in the spring. Today, seasonal flu is estimated to kill about 36,000 people in the United States each year, and half a million worldwide.

Yet the flu, in many important respects, remains mysterious. Determining how many deaths it really causes, or even who has it, is no simple matter. We think we have the flu anytime we fall ill with an ailment that brings on headache, malaise, fever, coughing, sneezing, and that achy feeling as if we've been sleeping on a bed of rocks, but researchers have found that at most half, and perhaps as few as 7 or 8 percent, of such cases are actually caused by an influenza virus in any given year. More than 200 known viruses and other pathogens can cause the suite of symptoms known as "influenza-like illness"; respiratory syncytial virus, bocavirus, coronavirus, and rhinovirus are just a few of the bugs that can make a person feel rotten. And depending on the season, in up to two-thirds of the cases of flu-like illness, no cause at all can be found.

Nobody knows precisely why we are much more likely to catch the flu in the winter months than at other times of the year. Perhaps it's because flu viruses flourish in cool temperatures and are killed by exposure to sunlight. Or maybe it's because in winter, people spend more time indoors, where a sneeze or a cough can more easily spread a virus to others. What is certain is that influenza viruses mutate with amazing speed, so each flu season sees slightly different genetic versions of the viruses that infected people the year before. Every year, the World Health Organization [WHO] and the Centers for Disease Control and Prevention [CDC] collect data from 94 nations on the flu viruses that circulated the previous year, and then make an educated guess about which viruses are likely to circulate in the coming fall. Based on that information, the U.S. Food and Drug Administration issues orders to manufacturers in February for a vaccine that includes the three most likely strains.

The flu, in many important respects, remains mysterious.

Flu Pandemics

Every once in a while, however, a very different bug pops up and infects far more people than the normal seasonal flu variants do. It is these novel viruses that are responsible for pandemics, defined by the World Health Organization as events that occur when "a new influenza virus appears against which the human population has no immunity" and which can sweep around the world in a very short time. The worst flu pandemic in recorded history was the "Spanish flu" of 1918–19, at the end of World War I. A third of the world's population was infected, with at least 40 million and perhaps as many as 100 million people dying—more than were killed in World Wars I and II combined. (Some scholars suggest that one reason World War I ended was that so many soldiers were sick or dying from flu.) Since then, two other flu pandemics have occurred, in 1957 and 1968, neither of which was particularly lethal.

In August [2009], the President's Council of Advisors on Science and Technology projected that this fall and winter, the swine flu, H1N1, could infect anywhere between one-third and one-half of the U.S. population and could kill as many as 90,000 Americans, two and a half times the number killed in a typical flu season. But precisely how deadly, or even how infectious, this year's H1N1 pandemic will turn out to be won't be known until it's over [the CDC estimates that the 2009 H1N1 virus killed between 8,870 and 18,300 Americans]. Most reports coming from the Southern Hemisphere in late August (the end of winter there) suggested that the swine flu is highly infectious, but not particularly lethal. For example, Australian officials estimated they would finish winter with under 1,000 swine flu deaths—fewer than the usual 1,500 to 3,000 from seasonal flu. Among those who have died in the U.S., about 70 percent were already suffering from congenital conditions like cerebral palsy or underlying illnesses such as cancer, asthma, or AIDS, which make people more vulnerable.

Today, flu vaccine is a staple of public-health policy; in a normal year, some 100 million Americans get vaccinated.

The Flu Vaccine

Public-health officials consider vaccine their most formidable defense against the pandemic—indeed, against any flu—and on the surface, their faith seems justified. Vaccines developed over the course of the 20th century slashed the death rates of nearly a dozen infectious diseases, such as smallpox and polio, and vaccination became one of medicine's most potent weapons. Influenza virus was first identified in the 1930s, and by the mid-1940s, researchers had produced a vaccine that was given to soldiers in World War II. The U.S. government got serious about promoting flu vaccine after the 1957 flu pandemic brought home influenza's continuing potential to cause widespread illness and death. Today, flu vaccine is a staple of public-health policy; in a normal year, some 100 million Americans get vaccinated.

But while vaccines for, say, whooping cough and polio clearly and dramatically reduced death rates from those diseases, the impact of flu vaccine has been harder to determine. Flu comes and goes with the seasons, and often it does not kill people directly, but rather contributes to death by making the body more susceptible to secondary infections like pneumonia or bronchitis. For this reason, researchers studying the impact of flu vaccination typically look at deaths from all causes during flu season, and compare the vaccinated and unvaccinated populations.

Such comparisons have shown a dramatic difference in mortality between these two groups: study after study has found that people who get a flu shot in the fall are about half as likely to die that winter—from any cause—as people who do not. Get your flu shot each year, the literature suggests, and you will dramatically reduce your chance of dying during flu season.

People who choose to be vaccinated may differ in many important respects from people who go unvaccinated—and those differences can influence the chance of death during flu season.

Mortality Reduction by Vaccination

Yet in the view of several vaccine skeptics, this claim is suspicious on its face. Influenza causes only a small minority of all deaths in the U.S., even among senior citizens, and even after adding in the deaths to which flu might have contributed indirectly. When researchers from the National Institute of Allergy and Infectious Diseases included all deaths from illnesses that flu aggravates, like lung disease or chronic heart failure, they found that flu accounts for, at most, 10 percent of winter deaths among the elderly. So how could flu vaccine possibly reduce total deaths by half? Tom Jefferson, a physician based in Rome and the head of the Vaccines Field at the Cochrane Collaboration, a highly respected international network of researchers who appraise medical evidence, says: "For a vaccine to reduce mortality by 50 percent and up to 90 percent in some studies means it has to prevent deaths not just from influenza, but also from falls, fires, heart disease, strokes, and car accidents. That's not a vaccine, that's a miracle."

The estimate of 50 percent mortality reduction is based on "cohort studies," which compare death rates in large groups, or cohorts, of people who choose to be vaccinated, against death rates in groups who don't. But people who choose to be vaccinated may differ in many important respects from people who go unvaccinated—and those differences can influence the chance of death during flu season. Education, lifestyle, income, and many other "confounding" factors can come into play, and as a result, cohort studies are notoriously prone to bias. When researchers crunch the numbers, they typically try to factor out variables that could bias the results, but, as Jefferson remarks, "you can adjust for the confounders you know about, not for the ones you don't," and researchers can't always anticipate what factors are likely to be important to whether a patient dies from flu. There is always the chance that they might miss some critical confounder that renders their results entirely wrong.

A Controversial Study

When Lisa Jackson, a physician and senior investigator with the Group Health Research Center, in Seattle [Washington], began wondering aloud to colleagues if maybe something was amiss with the estimate of 50 percent mortality reduction for people who get flu vaccine, the response she got sounded more like doctrine than science. "People told me, 'No good can come of [asking] this,'" she says. "'Potentially a lot of bad could happen' for me professionally by raising any criticism that might dissuade people from getting vaccinated, because of course, 'We know that vaccine works.' This was the prevailing wisdom."

Nonetheless, in 2004, Jackson and three colleagues set out to determine whether the mortality difference between the vaccinated and the unvaccinated might be caused by a phenomenon known as the "healthy user effect." They hypothesized that on average, people who get vaccinated are simply healthier than those who don't, and thus less liable to die over the short term. People who don't get vaccinated may be bedridden or otherwise too sick to go get a shot. They may also be more likely to succumb to flu or any other illness, because they are generally older and sicker. To test their thesis, Jackson and her colleagues combed through eight years of medical data on more than 72,000 people 65 and older. They looked at who got flu shots and who didn't. Then they examined which group's members were more likely to die of any cause when it was *not* flu season.

Jackson's findings showed that *outside of flu season*, the baseline risk of death among people who did not get vaccinated was approximately 60 percent higher than among those who did, lending support to the hypothesis that on average, healthy people chose to get the vaccine, while the "frail elderly" didn't or couldn't. In fact, the healthy-user effect explained the entire benefit that other researchers were attributing to flu vaccine, suggesting that the vaccine itself might not reduce mortality at all. Jackson's papers "are beautiful," says Lone Simonsen, who is a professor of global health at George Washington University, in Washington, D.C., and an internationally recognized expert in influenza and vaccine epidemiology. "They are classic studies in epidemiology, they are so carefully done."

The results were also so unexpected that many experts simply refused to believe them. Jackson's papers were turned down for publication in the top-ranked medical journals. One flu expert who reviewed her studies for the *Journal of the American Medical Association* wrote, "To accept these results would be to say that the earth is flat!" When the papers were finally published in 2006, in the less prominent *International Journal of Epidemiology*, they were largely ignored by doctors and public-health officials. "The answer I got," says Jackson, "was not the right answer."

Rising rates of vaccination of the elderly over the past two decades have not coincided with a lower overall mortality rate.

Vaccination and Mortality Rates

The history of flu vaccination suggests other reasons to doubt claims that it dramatically reduces mortality. In 2004, for example, vaccine production fell behind, causing a 40 percent drop in immunization rates. Yet mortality did not rise. In addition, vaccine "mismatches" occurred in 1968 and 1997: in both years, the vaccine that had been produced in the summer protected against one set of viruses, but come winter, a different set was circulating. In effect, nobody was vaccinated. Yet death rates from all causes, including flu and the various illnesses it can exacerbate, did not budge. Sumit Majumdar, a physician and researcher at the University of Alberta, in Canada, offers another historical observation: rising rates of vaccination of the elderly over the past two decades have not coincided with a lower overall mortality rate. In 1989, only 15 percent of people over age 65 in the U.S. and Canada were vaccinated against flu. Today, more than 65 percent are immunized. Yet death rates among the elderly during flu season have increased rather than decreased.

Vaccine proponents call Majumdar's last observation an "ecological fallacy," because he fails, in their view, to consider changes in the larger environment that could have boosted death rates over the years—even as rising vaccination rates were doing their part to keep mortality in check. The proponents suggest, for instance, that influenza viruses may have become more contagious over time, and thus are infecting greater numbers of elderly people, including some who have been vaccinated. Or maybe the viruses are becoming more lethal. Or maybe the elderly have less immunity to flu than they once did because, say, their diets have changed.

Or maybe vaccine just doesn't prevent deaths in the elderly. Of course, that's the one possibility that vaccine adherents won't consider. Nancy Cox, the CDC's influenza division chief, says flatly, "The flu vaccine is the best way to protect against flu." Anthony Fauci, a physician and the director of the National Institute of Allergy and Infectious Diseases at the NIH [National Institutes of Health], where much of the basic science of flu vaccine has been worked out, says, "I have no doubt that it is effective in conferring some degree of protection. To say otherwise is a minority view."

Majumdar says, "We keep coming up against the belief that we've reduced mortality by 50 percent," and when researchers poke holes in the evidence, "people pound the pulpit." . . .

A Question of Efficacy

Demonstrating the efficacy (or lack thereof) of vaccine and antivirals during flu season would not be hard to do, given the proper resources. Take a group of people who are at risk of getting the flu, and randomly assign half to get the vaccine and the other half a dummy shot. Then count the people in each group who come down with flu, suffer serious illness, or die. (A similarly designed trial would suffice for the antivirals.) It might sound coldhearted, but it is the only way to know for certain whether, and for whom, current remedies actually work. It would also be useful to know whether vaccinating healthy people—who can mount an immune response on their own—protects the more vulnerable people around them. For example, immunizing nursing-home staff and healthy children is thought to reduce the spread of flu to the elderly and the immune-compromised. Pinning down the effectiveness of this strategy would be a bit more complex, but not impossible.

In the absence of such evidence, we are left with two possibilities. One is that flu vaccine is in fact highly beneficial, or at least helpful. Solid evidence to that effect would encourage more citizens—and particularly more health professionals—to get their shots and prevent the flu's spread. As it stands, more than 50 percent of health-care workers say they do not intend to get vaccinated for swine flu and don't routinely get their shots for seasonal flu, in part because many of them doubt the vaccines' efficacy. The other possibility, of course, is that we're relying heavily on vaccines and antivirals that simply don't work, or don't work as well as we believe. And as a result, we may be neglecting other, proven measures that could minimize the death rate during pandemics.

The Neglect of Alternate Measures

"Vaccines give us a false sense of security," says Sumit Majumdar. "When you have a strategy that [everybody thinks] reduces death by 50 percent, it's pretty hard to invest resources to come up with better remedies." For instance, health departments in every state are responsible for submitting plans to the CDC for educating the public, in the event of a serious pandemic, about hand-washing and "social distancing" (voluntary quarantines, school closings, and even enforcement of mandatory quarantines to keep infected people in their homes). Putting these plans into action will require considerable coordination among government officials, the media, and health-care workers—and widespread buy-in from the public. Yet little discussion has appeared in the press to help people understand the measures they can take to best protect themselves during a flu outbreak—other than vaccination and antivirals.

"Launched early enough and continued long enough, social distancing can blunt the impact of a pandemic," says Howard Markel, a pediatrician and historian of medicine at the University of Michigan. Washing hands diligently, avoiding public places during an outbreak, and having a supply of canned goods and water on hand are sound defenses, he says. Such steps could be highly effective in helping to slow the spread of the virus. In Mexico, for instance, where the first swine flu cases were identified in March, the government launched an aggressive program to get people to wash their hands and exhorted those who were sick to stay home and effectively quarantine themselves. In the United Kingdom, the national health department is promoting a "buddy" program, encouraging citizens to find a friend or neighbor willing to deliver food and medicine so people who fall ill can stay home.

In the absence of better evidence, vaccines and antivirals must be viewed as only partial and uncertain defenses against the flu.

A Possible Illusion

In the U.S., by contrast, our reliance on vaccination may have the opposite effect: breeding feelings of invulnerability, and leading some people to ignore simple measures like better-than-normal hygiene, staying away from those who are sick, and staying home when they feel ill. Likewise, our encouragement of early treatment with antiviral drugs will likely lead many people to show up at the hospital at first sniffle. "There's no worse place to go than the hospital during flu season," says Majumdar. Those who don't have the flu are more likely to catch it there, and those who do will spread it around, he says. "But we don't tell people this."

All of which leaves open the question of what people should do when faced with a decision about whether to get themselves and their families vaccinated. There is little immediate danger from getting a seasonal flu shot, aside from a sore arm and mild flu-like symptoms. The safety of the swine flu vaccine remains to be seen. In the absence of better evidence, vaccines and antivirals must be viewed as only partial and uncertain defenses against the flu. And they may be mere talismans. By being afraid to do the proper studies now, we may be condemning ourselves to using treatments based on illusion and faith rather than sound science.

Do the Benefits of Vaccines Outweigh Possible Harms?

Overview: Fear of Vaccines

Amanda Gardner

Amanda Gardner is a reporter for HealthDay, a health news website.

As long as vaccinations against disease have been around, there have been die-hard opponents convinced that these shots do more harm than good.

A Resurgence of Vaccine Phobia

This type of "vaccine phobia" has perhaps never been expressed more vehemently than with the standard measles-mumps-rubella (MMR) childhood vaccine, which many insist is tied to autism.

Even after the retraction last year [2010] by *The Lancet* of the controversial study that first proposed such a link, and subsequent charges of fraud against its lead author, 18 percent of Americans surveyed in a recent *Harris Interactive/HealthDay* poll said they believed the MMR shot could cause autism.

Why are vaccines such lightning rods for suspicion and fear, despite scientific evidence that immunization campaigns have helped millions of people around the world live longer, healthier lives? One thing is for sure: the trend is not a new one.

According to a recent article in the *New England Journal of Medicine*, fear of vaccinations has been around since Edward Jenner administered his first smallpox shot in 1796. Skepticism waned during the middle of the 20th century, however, as the first large-scale immunization campaigns beat back longtime killers such as diphtheria, tetanus, polio and measles.

And yet early in the 21st century, fear of vaccines has reared up once more. A study published in the March 2010 issue of *Pediatrics* found that although 90 percent of surveyed parents still thought vaccines offered good protection for their kids, almost 12 percent had refused at least one vaccine for their child.

The Cost of Vaccine Fears

These fears come at a real cost to public health, experts say: Declines in vaccination rates have been tied to recent U.S. outbreaks of measles and whooping cough, potentially fatal diseases the shots were meant to prevent.

Early in the 21st century, fear of vaccines has reared up once more.

Doctors have noted the trend, even among adult patients.

"I have been increasingly frustrated with efforts to vaccinate people in my clinic and how my persuasion efforts, which are formidable, are not working," said Dr. Len Horovitz, a pulmonary specialist with Lenox Hill Hospital in New York City.

"There's a mythology surrounding vaccinations," Horovitz said. It's not always logical, since some patients refuse "to put anything foreign [like a vaccine] in their body," even as they puff away on cigarettes, he added.

And vaccines seem especially singled out for distrust—few people suspect other common therapies, such as cough syrups or antibiotics, of causing autism or other illnesses in kids. So why the lingering suspicion, despite so much solid science suggesting vaccines are both safe and lifesaving?

The Successes of Vaccines

According to experts, one reason may be that immunization campaigns have become victims of their own successes.

"We're not seeing these [infectious] diseases any more," said Dr. Paul Offit, chief of infectious diseases and director of the Vaccine Education Center at Children's Hospital of Philadelphia. "For my parents and me, vaccines were an easy sell. I had measles, mumps, chickenpox. Fortunately, I didn't have polio, but I could have."

In generations past, the overwhelming benefits of vaccination were easy to spot as the numbers of children killed or disabled by infectious disease trickled away.

"We actually had an incident during the 1950s where the vaccine [in rare cases] may have caused polio," noted Dr. Max Wiznitzer, a child neurologist with Rainbow Babies & Children's Hospital, University Hospitals Case Medical Center in Cleveland. "Do you think people cared? They were so scared of polio that they kept lining up [for the shot]."

"In today's day and age that would never fly," he continued. "We're not seeing the natural infections any more, therefore we have a skewed view of the benefits and risks."

The Concern of Parents

The fear seems also to have been fueled by an ever expanding and complicated vaccine schedule for younger children, with the U.S. Centers for Disease Control and Prevention now recommending 11 vaccines in multiple doses during the first six years of life.

All of that can play into parents' natural protective instincts for their children, Wiznitzer said. "Families always worry about their children's health, so if a claim comes up that vaccines could impact on their child's health, they worry."

In many parents' minds, more vaccinations must imply a higher potential for something untoward happening, and thus the wider benefits of immunization become overshadowed by that concern.

Also lying at the heart of things may be the simple fact that people are afraid of needles penetrating their bodies, or their children's bodies.

Unlike pills, for example, "shots are considered invasive. It's an aggressive act," explained Offit, who has just written a book, *Deadly Choices: How the Anti-Vaccine Movement Threatens Us All.* "A child is taken against their will, pinned down on a table or held by their mother. It can hurt and children can get as many as 26 inoculations in the first six years of life. People don't understand what's in the vial. [To them] it's just some kind of biological agent."

Barbara Loe Fisher is co-founder and president of the National Vaccine Information Center, which supports more research into the safety of vaccinations. In an interview for the *Harris Interactive/HealthDay* poll story, she said autism is just one concern linked to vaccines.

"Parents have legitimate questions about vaccine risks and want better vaccine science to define those risks for their own child," Fisher said. "This concern long predated the debate about vaccines and autism."

Concerns About Vaccine Safety Are Out of Proportion to Actual Risk

National Network for Immunization Information

The National Network for Immunization Information is an affiliation of several medical groups whose goal is to provide the public, health professionals, policymakers, and the media with up-to-date, scientifically valid information related to immunization.

Decades ago, when thousands of children and adults in the United States contracted smallpox, diphtheria, poliomyelitis or measles each year, vaccine safety concerns were not very common. People were more afraid of the diseases themselves than of possible side effects of the vaccines. Because of the success of vaccines, the situation is very different today: the diseases aren't feared and concerns about vaccine safety are common.

Public Knowledge About Vaccines

Fortunately, the majority of parents understand the benefits of immunizations. But it is hard for some to appreciate risks that they don't see. For example, most parents today have never seen a child paralyzed by polio, or choking to death from diphtheria, or brain damaged by measles. As a consequence, fear of these diseases does not—but should—haunt parents as it did historically.

It is also difficult to understand the importance of new vaccines that target illnesses that many know little about, like a vaccine to prevent infection by the sexually-transmitted human papillomaviruses (HPV). Looking at an innocent 10 year old, it is hard to imagine her being sexually active, much less her being at risk of cervical cancer decades later because she wasn't vaccinated against HPV, a common infection that causes no symptoms.

While no vaccine is 100% safe, serious side effects are rare. However, because many vaccines are given to children at the ages when developmental and other problems are first being recognized, some parents may think that vaccines are to blame—it is difficult to grasp that the coincidence of timing does not mean that the vaccine caused the problem.

To compound the problem, the media carries stories about children whose parents believe that their child has been harmed by a vaccine, naturally causing concerns among other parents. And then, when parents try to get more information on the Internet, their concerns can be further heightened because the information they find may seem reasonable—but may be very wrong.

When an unimmunized child develops a vaccine-preventable disease, the child gets all the risks of that disease.

Vaccine-Preventable Diseases

Although we personally don't see them very often, these illnesses are very much waiting for an opportunity to return. Except for smallpox (for which we no longer give vaccine), the vaccine-preventable diseases are still here. For example, tetanus—which does not spread from person-to-person—is still in the soil; cases of mumps and rubella (and congenital rubella) continue to occur; and measles—the most contagious disease—is active many places in the world, often arriving in our midst by airplane.

When an unimmunized child develops a vaccine-preventable disease, the child gets all the risks of that disease: 1–4 per thousand will die from measles, half will die from tetanus, 1–2 per hundred will develop paralytic polio, and so on.

Much of the protection against vaccine-preventable diseases that we have in our country is because so many children are immunized. Having many immunized children indirectly protects those who cannot get [the] vaccine and protects those children for whom the vaccine didn't work—because no vaccine protects 100% of those who get it. Indirect protection occurs because susceptible children are not exposed to the disease-causing agents.

For example, in 2008 three unimmunized children in Minnesota developed invasive disease due to *Haemophilus influenzae* type B (Hib) infection. One of the children died. Two other children who also developed invasive Hib disease should have been protected by community immunity, but were not— one was too young to be immune from vaccine and the other had a congenital immune deficiency.

That is why we need to continue giving vaccines, even if we don't see the diseases they prevent. To not immunize a child can have tragic consequences for the child, the child's family, and for the child's classmates and friends.

Vaccine Safety Concerns and Risk Perception

No vaccine is 100% effective; no vaccine is 100% safe. As with any drug, there are risks and side effects with vaccines, although serious side effects are rare. However, there is a much higher standard of safety expected of preventive vaccines than for drugs because vaccines are given to many people most of whom are healthy.

For example, people tolerate far less risk from the vaccine used to prevent infection with *Haemophilus influenzae* type b than they do the antibiotics that are used to treat the infections it causes.

Research shows that people respond better to some types of risks than others. Natural risks (such as infections for which there are no vaccines) are better tolerated than manmade risks (such as vaccine side effects). Also, risks that affect adults are better tolerated than risks affecting our children. Risks that are perceived to have unclear benefits may be less tolerated than risks where the benefits are understood.

For example, because measles, mumps and rubella (MMR) are no longer epidemic in the United States, some parents incorrectly assume that the risks of contracting the diseases are lower than the risk of their child experiencing an adverse reaction to MMR vaccine. They conclude that there may be little benefit from immunizing their child, hence there may seem to be no reason to take the risk of an adverse event. However, serious side effects from the MMR vaccine are rare—but there have been introductions of measles from other countries, cases of rubella and a large outbreak of mumps in 2006. These infections remain a risk to children and communities; many are "just a plane ride away".

Many are unaware that their community is at risk for exposure to the vaccine-preventable diseases.

Perception of risk depends on people's experiences and knowledge. A person who experienced an adverse event after vaccination—or thinks that they know someone who did—will perceive vaccines as riskier than a person who has not. Conversely, one who has survived a vaccine-preventable disease—or a physician who has had to treat that disease—will likely be an advocate for vaccines.

Many vaccines are given to children at the ages when developmental and other problems are being recognized for the first time. Because something happened at about the same time that a vaccine was given, does not mean that one caused the other.

The Issue of Missing Information

Information may be available but that information may be unknown. Families need to be aware of the risks of exposure to infection, the importance of the proportion of children who are immune, and what the actual risks of complications from the different infections are. Without this information, families are uninformed and may develop a false sense of security and regard immunizations as unimportant.

For example, many are unaware that their community is at risk for exposure to the vaccine-preventable diseases. Others may not realize that their child could become ill if exposed to a vaccine-preventable disease—even if their child has received the vaccine.

In contrast to the uninformed, needed information may just not exist. For example, when a vaccine safety concern is first suggested, the necessary data to support or reject the hypothesis may not yet have been collected—in fact sometimes this may take several years of research.

The experience concerning the concern that thimerosal in vaccines might cause autism—first suggested in 1999—is illustrative of this. In 2001, when the Institute of Medicine's Immunization Safety Review Committee first examined the issue, there was little data available about exposure to thimerosal in vaccines among children who subsequently were recognized as being autistic. Thus the Committee was unable to say that there was no such association. By 2004, however, much more scientific data was available and the IOM Committee concluded that there was no association between vaccines and autism.

The Problem of Misinformation

The uninformed person can unwittingly spread misinformation. However, there are also intentional misinformers, who actively seek to mislead others.

Unfortunately, the timing and widespread use of vaccines make them easy scapegoats to be blamed for all sorts of serious illnesses, particularly those diseases that are poorly understood. Of course not all vaccine safety concerns are misinformation—only those that persist despite the evidence against them.

Misinformation tends to rely on emotion-filled stories about bad things that happened to children or were first recognized—coincidental in time with vaccine administration. Misinformation is often presented with distorted or misquoted scientific studies.

Many media stories use faulty reports and parental concerns to depict a "controversy" about vaccines, failing to mention that the scientific community does not feel that a controversy exists. For example, in spite of the substantial evidence now available that allows rejection of the hypotheses that vaccines cause autism, there are some who continue to state that they do. These claims now fall into the category of misinformation but may continue to be portrayed in media stories as 'controversies'.

In addition to a child's personal risk, the unimmunized child puts all children at risk.

The Unimmunized Child

The unimmunized child is at risk from vaccine preventable diseases. For example, a couple in Tennessee, confused about vaccine safety because of what they had read on the Internet, decided to delay their daughter's vaccinations. Some time later, the baby girl was stricken with a form of meningitis that could have been prevented by a vaccine.

In addition to a child's personal risk, the unimmunized child puts all children at risk because unimmunized children are more likely to acquire—and they are more likely to spread—vaccine preventable diseases within the community.

This is the reason why all parents should be concerned when other parents do not have their children fully immunized.

Concerns About a Link Between Vaccines and Autism Are Unfounded

John E. Calfee

John E. Calfee was a resident scholar at the American Enterprise Institute until his death in 2011.

Vaccines occupy an odd place in medical history. They are almost universally recognized as among the most valuable and cost-effective medical tools ever developed. The very first vaccine—for smallpox—curtailed and finally eradicated the most devastating infectious disease ever to strike humanity. The list of lifesaving vaccines developed in the past century or so is long. Most of them are especially protective for diseases that hit children the hardest, such as polio, measles, mumps, whooping cough, and diphtheria.

The Concern About Vaccine Safety

Yet vaccines have also been controversial, starting with the smallpox vaccine. Paul Offit, a noted vaccine researcher at the Children's Hospital of Philadelphia and the University of Pennsylvania, just published a book recounting the history of vaccine controversies and anti-vaccine movements in the United States and England. Partly history and partly a critical assessment of science and policy, it supplies essential guideposts for recent events.

Vaccine debates are sometimes about mandates, such as the requirement that children be vaccinated before starting school. But usually the issue is safety. At first glance, this makes little sense. Vaccines are tested on thousands or tens of thousands of patients, and because they are typically given to healthy persons, dangerous side effects are easy to spot, even when they are quite rare. Safety controversies usually focus on children, however, because millions of children are vaccinated every year at ages when several worrisome illnesses tend to arrive.

Occasionally, a new vaccine causes problems. This happened a decade or so ago with a vaccine for rotavirus. The vaccine kept children from being infected by a common virus that sometimes causes life-threatening dehydration, but the vaccine turned out to have a rare and dangerous side effect (a vaccine without that side effect has since received approval). Almost always, though, careful examination of huge databases makes clear that when an illness strikes soon after vaccination, it is almost always a coincidence.

Vaccines and Autism

In recent years, the biggest vaccine controversy by far has been over autism, which, yes, typically reveals itself in children at an age when vaccination is common. Offit wrote a book on this, too.

But some news this month [January 2011] requires a bit of background information.

A seminal event in the vaccine-autism controversy was the 1998 publication of an article in *The Lancet*, an old and prestigious medical journal in [Great] Britain. Coauthored by Andrew Wakefield and 12 others, the article reported on an examination of 12 children who had developed both gastrointestinal problems and severe behavioral problems after receiving the measles, mumps, and rubella (MMR) vaccine. Nine of the children had become autistic. The authors concluded that they had identified a new syndrome involving "colitis and pervasive developmental disorder," which they surmised but had yet to demonstrate was caused by the MMR vaccine.

Although immediately criticized as scientifically implausible, the article nevertheless created a firestorm—as did its flamboyant lead author. Ever since, the Wakefield *Lancet* article has been the single most prominent weapon in attacks on vaccines as a cause of autism. Among its consequences was that MMR vaccination in England dropped to dangerously low levels.

In recent years, the biggest vaccine controversy by far has been over autism.

Investigation of the Autism-Vaccine Link

The Wakefield article cried out for close scrutiny, which it eventually received. Investigative reporting by Brian Deer, a British journalist, has played a crucial role. Starting in early 2004, Deer's reports for the *Sunday Times* (of London) and a television network revealed numerous troubling details about the Wakefield study, including that Wakefield, some of his coauthors, and some patients in the study were involved in liability litigation against vaccine firms, that some of Wakefield's research was funded via the plaintiff bar, and that subjects were recruited in a non-scientific manner.

In its response to the first wave of Deer's reporting, *The Lancet* issued a statement on February 23, 2004, that reaffirmed the article's methods and conclusions but expressed regret that the editors had not been informed of an obvious conflict of interest. More telling, ten of Wakefield's coauthors published a brief "retraction of an interpretation" in *The Lancet* on March 6, 2004, in which they disavowed any conclusion that the MMR vaccine had been shown by their study to cause autism.

In the meantime, Deer continued his own investigation, publishing and otherwise communicating his findings to interested parties. In due course, the U.K.'s [United Kingdom's]

General Medical Council (GMC) conducted lengthy hearings into the study and the actions of Wakefield and his coauthors. These revealed, among other things, that the children in the study had been put through painful and dangerous procedures with scant notice, warning, or scientific justification.

Last May [2010], the GMC revoked Wakefield's medical license. He has since moved to Texas, where he operates an autism clinic that, according to Offit's autism book, offers treatments that involve substantial risks to patients but no prospect of benefit.

Last February, *The Lancet* finally retracted the article, not on scientific grounds but because of inadequate handling of the subjects in the study. This half-hearted retraction essentially left the study's conclusions in place. Long before, however, a series of studies (summarized in Offit's two books) had failed to replicate Wakefield's results and in fact had ruled out any connection between autism and any vaccine, including the MMR vaccine.

A Fraudulent Study

And, now, the final chapter.

On January 5 [2011], another U.K. medical journal—*BMJ*, formerly known as the *British Medical Journal*—posted the first of a series of articles by Deer in which Wakefield's article was revealed as being not merely sloppy or deceptively presented, but fraudulent. In combing through voluminous records in the Wakefield hearings plus other sources, Deer had found pervasive manipulation of basic data. For example, some of the subjects had behavioral symptoms before vaccination, post-vaccination data were misrepresented, and only one subject had regressive autism, the main condition at issue. Data for all 12 subjects had been manipulated in one way or another, always in a manner that favored the autism hypothesis.

In an accompanying editorial, the journal's editor-in-chief and two other editors endorsed these conclusions while also asking probing questions about, among other things, editorial oversight at *The Lancet*, a topic that *BMJ* will address in articles to be published shortly.

The denouement of the Wakefield scandal held few, if any, surprises for the scientists who have followed it most closely. But for the rest of us, a few remarks are in order on the entire vaccine controversy.

As Offit has pointed out in interviews, this latest finding will do little to deter those who think vaccines cause autism. They will always find plausible arguments for their cause and will receive support from a small coterie of physicians.

One has to wonder about *The Lancet*, however. One would have expected the editors to have fully retracted the article when its dubious provenance was first revealed. When a complete retraction finally came in February 2010, its tortured wording mainly suggested embarrassment, as if the editors already knew that the article was disreputable but did not want to let it go until they had some new facts to lean on, which happened to be fresh information (from Deer) about the manner in which the subjects were recruited.

There is such a thing as junk science, and it has been at the middle of the anti-vaccine movement since its inception.

The Truth About Vaccines

More fundamentally, we can hope that these events will reinforce certain truths about the childhood vaccine market.

First, checks and balances are potent. Naturally overcautious, the Food and Drug Administration is a nearly insurmountable barrier between children and bad vaccines.

Second, there is such a thing as junk science, and it has been at the middle of the anti-vaccine movement since its inception.

Third, vaccines are not perfect, and they do sometimes have serious side effects. The National Vaccine Injury Compensation Program is designed to deal with that. If anything, it is too generous in the sense of assigning blame to vaccines for harms for which even a biological plausibility is weak at best.

Fourth, liability litigation is a terrible way to deal with vaccine safety. Indeed, the failure of the liability system in the childhood vaccine market in the mid-1980s is the reason the system was replaced by the National Vaccine Injury Compensation Program in 1986. The simple fact is that it is usually impossible for a jury to know whether a vaccine caused the harm at issue. That leaves sympathy for the victim as the dominant force. That arrangement nearly destroyed the childhood vaccine market in the 1980s.

Fifth, yes, there are good arguments to be made about vaccination mandates and the importance of "herd immunity," which provides protection to the unvaccinated if, and only if, enough people are vaccinated.

And finally, the most important truth by far: vaccines are still probably the most valuable medical tool ever invented, and the failure to use them would be a disaster of epic proportions.

Vaccines Are a Danger to Health

Russell L. Blaylock

Russell L. Blaylock is a board-certified neurosurgeon and author of The Blaylock Wellness Report.

People today face a massive, invasive assault against their well-being, and it begins at birth.

Children get 24 vaccines by age 1 and almost 40 by the time they start school. The medical authorities—the Centers for Disease Control and Prevention, the American Academy of Pediatrics, and the American Academy of Family Physicians—recommend as many as 150 vaccines during our lifetimes.

The Time Before Vaccines

Things were not always this way. When I was a child, we received just four vaccines. There were no vaccines for common childhood maladies, like measles, mumps, and chickenpox. Like my friends, I contracted most of these minor illnesses and of course got over them.

Despite what the vaccine scaremongers would have you believe, the streets were not filled with dead and dying children. Not a single child in any of my classes in grammar school, junior high, or high school developed a serious complication as a result of having any of the normal childhood diseases that parents are now urged to prevent through vaccination.

Medical journalist Neil Z. Miller has carefully researched the data on childhood deaths during the "scary days of unvaccinated children" in the U.S. and has uncovered some surprising facts:

- The death rate from measles fell more than 95 percent before mass measles vaccination began in the U.S. The same occurred in Great Britain.

- Whooping cough death rates were falling before mass vaccination programs began—by an eye-popping 75 percent in both countries.

- The death rate from the polio scourge was falling—well before the polio vaccine was introduced.

Why were the death rates from these childhood diseases falling so rapidly?

Pro-vaccine elements—the government and big pharma—take credit for that decline in death rates, but the truth is simpler: Better nutrition and sanitation, especially in big cities, account for most of the improvement in death statistics. This information has been noted in health literature but has been widely ignored.

This all-too-common abuse of statistics keeps the public convinced that the vaccine program has saved millions of lives.

Correlation and Causation

In the same way, proponents for fluoridating water have conned the public and most dentists into believing that adding fluoride to public water supplies has decreased the number of cavities. But those same improvements in nutrition and sanitation are also responsible for the dramatic fall in cavities.

In fact, cavity rates worldwide began to fall dramatically and to the same extent in both fluoridated and unfluoridated communities at exactly the same time. Why? Because of better nutrition in cities and a higher consumption of cheese, which is high in teeth-strengthening calcium. This has been confirmed in almost every study on the topic.

We are living cleaner, safer and more nutritious lives, but vaccines and fluoride simply happened at about the same time. As the statisticians say, correlation (two things happening at once) does not prove causation (one thing causes another).

This all-too-common abuse of statistics keeps the public convinced that the vaccine program has saved millions of lives. It also instills an insidious fear that any change in the program will bring back the mythical days of children dying in droves.

The Use of Scare Tactics

I have heard testimony from hundreds of mothers who say they agreed to vaccination only because a pediatrician scared them into it. These scare stories, especially those that warn of impending waves of mass fatalities, are not based on hard science—or even firsthand experience. Instead, doctors make their case using figures culled from impoverished, Third-World countries with high rates of malnutrition, parasitic infections, and poor-to-non-existent sanitation.

Meanwhile, the most cursory review of medical history shows that virtually every case of pandemic death followed a period of widespread poor nutrition. For example, the influenza pandemic of 1917 occurred on the heels of the devastation of World War I.

Medical professionals use the same scare tactic to tell parents that they must vaccinate their newborns against hepatitis B.

The fact is, the vast majority of babies are at absolutely no risk from this disease. Only mothers who are infected with the virus during pregnancy put their children at risk.

Even then, the majority will not transfer the virus to their children. High-risk mothers are those who use intravenous drugs, have received tainted blood transfusions, or who have HIV infections.

Exaggerations About Disease

Vaccine authorities also know that hepatitis B infections in adults rarely result in liver failure, and the disease is basically harmless in more than 90 percent of cases. They also ignore the fact that the hepatitis B vaccine only protects for a few years, so they recommend booster vaccines every two years until 18, the age when a patient first faces any real risk from the disease.

Yet three times more children under 14 suffered serious vaccine reactions than the number who actually contract the disease itself.

The most blatant scare tactic is foisted on older folks. The number is horrifying: Supposedly, 36,000 elderly people die each year from the flu.

If true, then the same number of people die from the flu every year as died during some of the worst flu pandemics on record—impossible! Interestingly, there are no records kept of how many elderly die because of the flu vaccine, but this number may be in the thousands.

In this issue of *The Blaylock Wellness Report*, I will bring you key information about vaccine studies you will never hear from your doctor or the media—for reasons that might shock you.

Ultimate Protection Is Infection

Most people presume that taking a vaccine provides the same level of immunity as getting the disease. Actually, science proves the opposite.

A number of compelling studies show that when you contract a disease naturally—chickenpox, for instance—the immune system becomes very active, kills the virus and then quickly goes back into a resting state. These studies show that natural infections give a person lifelong immunity to the disease; no booster shots are needed.

Lifetime immunity! Compare that to vaccines. A growing number of studies show that, for many vaccines, the length of immunity following vaccination lasts no more than two to 10 years. Booster immunity lasts for even shorter periods, which is why you hear about the need for regular boosters.

Even worse, studies show that many of the vaccines, such as the mixed vaccine against measles, mumps and rubella (MMR) and *Haemophilus influenzae* type b (known as Hib), actually suppress immunity.

Asthma rates continue to climb, and it parallels the growing number of vaccines being given to children.

As a result, your child actually becomes more susceptible to infection by any number of viruses and bacteria. This is why mothers are warned to keep their freshly Hib-vaccinated children out of daycare centers, because their risk of developing a severe form of meningitis is actually higher for several weeks after they are given the vaccine than before being vaccinated.

Many vaccines, especially tetanus and DtaP, which is three vaccines mixed to immunize against diphtheria, whooping cough and tetanus, increase the risk of children developing asthma, eczema and even juvenile diabetes, which are autoimmune-related diseases.

Asthma rates continue to climb, and it parallels the growing number of vaccines being given to children. Likewise, mercury has been proven to induce autoimmune diseases in genetically susceptible people.

The Danger of Live Virus Vaccines

Some vaccines, including the MMR, smallpox, and chickenpox vaccines, contain live viruses. Manufacturers weaken the virus (thus they are called "attenuated" viruses) so that it, in theory, confers immunity rather than triggers the disease. Vaccine proponents assure the public that these vaccines are safe. Scientists are now beginning to question this assurance for many reasons:

- In some people the virus is not killed off. Instead, it is permanently imbedded in the person's internal organs. One autopsy study of elderly people dying of non-infectious diseases found live measles virus in 45 percent of cases in their body organs and in 20 percent of cases in their brains.

- Imbedded viruses (from the vaccines) were highly mutated, a reason for great concern. Virologists have noted that such mutated viruses can cause completely unrelated diseases. Instead of causing typical measles, for example, the mutated measles virus can cause multiple sclerosis, muscle pains, Crohn's disease, or brain degeneration. It appears that they become mutated by the masses of free radicals (destabilized molecules) we produce over a lifetime—in our own bodies.

- By giving three and sometimes four live viruses together, the risk of developing a lifetime viral infection (a persistent viral infection) increases tremendously. This is especially so with the MMR vaccine, which contains two live viruses known to suppress the immune system for months.

The Danger of Immune Suppression

That suppression effect is powerful. It resembles the immune suppression seen with the HIV virus associated with AIDS.

During this prolonged period of immune suppression, both adults and children will be much more likely to develop other infections. This means that your child might die from meningitis or chickenpox as a direct result of the vaccine—and not because not enough people vaccinated their children, as the vaccine proponents would have you think.

One virus a child might contract during the period of immune suppression is the cytomegalovirus, which commonly infects babies and small children whose immune systems are suppressed. This virus is strongly associated with carotid stenosis, which causes strokes in adults.

Adults who receive boosters with these immune-suppressing vaccines risk developing overwhelming infections from pathogenic bacteria, such as pneumococcus, streptococcus, and staphylococcus. Remember, pneumonia is a leading cause of death in severe flu cases.

Chronically sick elderly people are at a great risk of contracting viruses from children vaccinated with live viruses up to a month after that contact.

No one stops to think that the MMR vaccine will suppress the person's immunity and thereby increase the risk of getting meningitis.

Vaccines for College Students

College students are now told to get booster shots of MMR, as well as a human papillomavirus (HPV) series, chickenpox, meningococcal (meningitis) and a tetanus booster, if one has not been given in 10 years. That's nine vaccines immediately before starting college. Of these, most universities actually require the meningococcal, MMR, and chickenpox vaccines.

No one stops to think that the MMR vaccine will suppress the person's immunity and thereby increase the risk of getting meningitis. This may explain why the incidence of meningitis is higher only for students who live on campus.

College-age misbehavior also plays a role. The following increase the risk of meningitis:

- Binge drinking

- Street drugs

- A poor diet filled with immune-suppressing omega-6 oils (common in snack chips and fast foods)

- Extreme exhaustion caused by intense partying

Combine this with the profound immune suppression caused by the measles and rubella viruses used in the vaccines, and you have a prescription for disaster.

In the case of polio, there is direct evidence against live vaccines: There is conclusive proof that the live virus vaccine itself caused all cases of polio after 1965. Polio literally spread from vaccinated children to their parents, classmates, and neighbors.

Live virus vaccines should not be used, especially in immunosuppressed children and in older people. Studies have shown that weakened immune systems in children are much more common than previously thought, and that most doctors fail to recognize it.

Medical authorities agree that immune-suppressed people should not be vaccinated at all. Now we learn that the live virus vaccines themselves are a major cause of the condition.

A Frightening Vaccine Myth

Intelligent parents have asked their doctors, If I choose not to vaccinate my child, how would that endanger someone else's child? After all, if the vaccines are as effective as their advocates claim, one or two temporarily sick kids shouldn't be a danger to a child who has been vaccinated.

It's a reasonable question—and a major problem for the proponents of mass forced vaccination, until they hit upon the concept of "herd immunity."

The idea goes like this: You can effectively stop epidemics of contagious diseases if you immunize a "magical" number of the population. I say magical because it keeps changing. When first proposed in 1933, the magic number was 68 percent of the population. Then it became 80 percent and now it stands at 98 percent.

The higher the number, of course, the more vaccines are sold.

If you ask doctors why we have not had an epidemic of diphtheria or tetanus in the last 60 years, they would quickly reply "herd immunity."

Yet the largest segment of the population, the baby boomers, has not been immunized against childhood diseases since they were small children. That means that roughly half of the U.S. population has been without vaccine protection for these diseases for 50 years!

In essence, this nation has been without herd immunity protection for half a century, yet there has not been one mass outbreak of deadly childhood diseases. For more than a century, the Amish in this country have not vaccinated their children at all, and there has been no record of the wholesale deaths of Amish children.

Believe me, you would have heard about it.

Vaccine Failure Rates

Even more startling is the finding that when small outbreaks of whopping cough and measles do occur, the majority of affected children are found to have been vaccinated.

In the 1986 Kansas whooping cough outbreak, 90 percent of the affected children had been fully vaccinated. In the 1994 outbreak in Ohio, 82 percent had been vaccinated, and 74 percent of kids had their shots in the 1996 Vermont outbreak. I personally had whooping cough as a child after being given the vaccine that was supposed to prevent it.

This means that the majority of infections occur in fully vaccinated kids, not in those who have not been vaccinated. It also confirms that the herd immunity idea is a myth, since even the vaccinated children are not being protected.

Remember, for herd immunity to work the immunization has to be "successful," meaning that it has to prevent the disease. With vaccine failure rates varying from 35 percent to 90 percent, not many people have been "successfully" vaccinated.

A number of studies have shown that most vaccines lose their effectiveness within two to five years and that booster shots rarely last even two years. If you check the Centers for Disease Control site under vaccine schedules you will note that, if you were born before 1957, you do not need the MMR vaccine.

Why? Because those of us born before this time have life-long immunity to all childhood infections—because we were exposed to them.

When small outbreaks of whopping cough and measles do occur, the majority of affected children are found to have been vaccinated.

Increased Incidence of Disease

The truth is, experts know their vaccines are not giving most children protection, so blaming unvaccinated children for out-breaks gives them an excuse. In fact, several of the vaccines are associated with an increased incidence of the very diseases they were designed to prevent.

For example, the rubella vaccine was supposed to prevent physical birth defects in infants born to women infected during pregnancy with the rubella virus, commonly called German measles.

Incredibly, the number of cases of congenital rubella mal-formations increased after the vaccine was introduced in 1969. In 1966, for example, there were 11 cases reported nationwide and 10 cases in 1967, before the vaccine program started.

One year after the mass vaccination of pregnant women began, the incidence increased to 77 cases—a 600 percent increase. The incidence has remained high ever since.

Vaccination for measles simply shifted the incidence of infection to newborns and small babies, a time of life when health complications and the chances of death are greatly increased.

The idea of sick newborns then gave pediatricians and the American Academy of Pediatrics a new set of horror stories to justify forced vaccination programs, all the while never admitting that the vaccine program itself caused the problem to begin with.

When young girls catch measles naturally, they in turn are able to pass this immune protection on to their babies when they are older, both by antibody transfer through the placenta and by way of breast milk after giving birth.

Vaccination with MMR prevents girls from getting the measles, and it also keeps their immunity from being transferred to their future children, who are then born utterly unprotected. . . .

Vaccines, Contamination, and Cancer

Most people assume that vaccines are sterile and free from contamination. Nothing could be further from the truth.

For example, few among the general public are aware that the polio vaccines from the 1950s and 1960s were contaminated with a cancer-causing virus called SV-40. It is estimated that more than 100,000,000 people worldwide were infected.

Vaccine scientists scrambled to see if it was causing cancer in people. They began to do long-term studies on large populations of the vaccinated to see if incidences of cancer rose. Yet later evaluations of these same studies showed that the studies were designed to obscure any increase. Why? Because linking the vaccine and cancer would have devastated the entire vaccination program.

When the story broke in the 1960s, vaccine manufacturers initially assured the public that the SV-40 virus was harmless to humans. Yet they knew from the work of Dr. Bernice Eddy at the National Institutes of Health that this virus caused cancer in primates.

To this day, vaccine defenders declare there is no problem with the SV-40 contamination.

Nevertheless, studies led by Dr. Michele Carbone have conclusively shown that this virus is responsible for a number of human cancers, including mesothelioma and bone cancer. One study involving 58,000 women found a 13-fold higher risk in brain tumors in women vaccinated with the contaminated vaccine compared to those not exposed to the virus.

The polio vaccine, too, was contaminated with cytomegalovirus, which is associated with strokes.

One would think that vaccine sterility would improve with the passage of time but, in fact, it has gotten worse.

Recent studies of vaccines from a number of manufacturers who supply vaccines to U.S. citizens found them to be contaminated.

In one study, 60 percent of the vials were contaminated. One of the viruses found in the vaccines was the pestivirus, which is associated with severe brain birth defects. In addition, viral fragments (like viral DNA, RNA, and proteins) have been found in a number of vaccines. Vaccine proponents assure us there is no danger, but the science says otherwise.

A number of studies have shown that the viral and bacterial fragments can become incorporated in other microorganisms, creating entirely new viruses and bacteria. Some result in dementia and degeneration of the brain.

One would think that vaccine sterility would improve with the passage of time but, in fact, it has gotten worse. The main reason is that the communist Chinese have entered the biotechnology market. They are now one of the world's leading manufacturers, producing 41 of the vaccines used in this country. Soon, they will manufacture the great majority of vaccines.

CHAPTER 3

Should Certain Vaccinations Be Mandatory?

Chapter Preface

As of 2011, the US Centers for Disease Control and Prevention (CDC) recommends the general public receive vaccines for sixteen viruses and bacteria: hepatitis B, diphtheria, tetanus, acellular pertussis (whooping cough), polio, influenza, varicella (chickenpox), measles, mumps, rubella, *haemophilus influenzae* type b (Hib), pneumococcal, rotavirus, hepatitis A, meningococcal, and human papillomavirus (HPV). Because some vaccines are combined, there are twelve different vaccines to deliver immunity for these sixteen diseases. Because most require multiple doses, several dozen injections are recommended throughout childhood and into adulthood. After age 60, the CDC recommends a single dose of the vaccine for zoster (commonly known as shingles). Several of these recommended vaccines are relatively new: The hepatitis A and varicella vaccines first became available in 1995, the first rotavirus vaccine came out in 1998 (withdrawn in 1999 and replaced in 2006), and the HPV vaccine and zoster vaccine first became available in 2006.

The federal government merely recommends certain vaccines for the general public, but all fifty states have laws requiring mandatory vaccination for public school attendance. The first state law mandating vaccination for attendance at school was enacted in Massachusetts in 1855, in order to prevent smallpox transmission at school. The US Supreme Court upheld the right of states to enact mandatory vaccinations in *Jacobson v. Massachusetts* (1905) and rejected a challenge to school vaccination laws in *Zucht v. King* (1922). The current laws vary from state to state, with some offering more exemptions to the vaccine requirements than others.

As of 2011, all states allow exemptions to their school vaccination laws for medical reasons; all states except Mississippi and West Virginia allow exemptions for religious reasons; and twenty states allow exemptions based on unspecified personal belief. In the last two decades, public concern about the safety—and doubts about the necessity—of vaccines has increased, though many would argue that this increased concern does not reflect any actual threat. Researchers report an overall increase in nonmedical exemptions from 1 percent to 1.5 percent between 1999 and 2004. And in states that allow exemptions for personal belief, they report that exemptions jumped from 1 percent to 2.5 percent.

Outbreaks of measles, polio, pertussis, and rubella have been documented in areas with high rates of unvaccinated children, causing concern that certain diseases believed to have been eliminated are making a comeback, placing at risk those who are not fully vaccinated or who cannot be vaccinated for medical reasons. The debate about mandatory vaccination laws continues. Disagreement abounds about the harms and benefits of vaccinations, and there are divergent views about the rights of individuals to make health care choices that may have an impact on others in the community.

Mandatory Vaccinations with Few Exceptions Are Necessary for Public Health

Pediatric Infectious Diseases Society

The Pediatric Infectious Diseases Society is an organization of medical professionals dedicated to the treatment, control, and eradication of infectious diseases affecting children.

The Pediatric Infectious Diseases Society is the world's largest organization of individuals dedicated to the treatment, control, and eradication of infectious diseases in children. As such, and given the background and rationale outlined below, the society opposes any legislation or regulation that would allow children to be exempted from mandatory immunizations based simply on their parents', or, in the case of adolescents, their own, secular personal beliefs.

Exemptions to Vaccine Mandates

It is recognized that in some states, failure to pass personal belief exemption legislation or regulation could result in public backlash that will erode support for immunization mandates. If legislation or regulation is being considered in this situation, it should contain the following provisions, which are intended to minimize use of exemptions as the "path of least resistance" for children who are behind on immunizations (whereby it would be easier to obtain an exemption than to catch-up the child's immunizations):

- The personal belief against immunization must be sincere and firmly held.

- Before a child is granted an exemption, the parents or guardians must receive state-approved counseling that delineates the personal and public health importance of immunization, the scientific basis for safety of vaccines, and the consequences of exemption for their child as well as other children in the community who are vulnerable to disease and cannot otherwise be protected.

- Before a child is granted an exemption, the parents or guardians must sign a statement that delineates the basis, strength, and duration of their belief; their understanding of the risks that refusal to immunize has on their child's health and the health of others (including the potential for serious illness or death); and their acknowledgement that they are making the decision not to vaccinate on behalf of their child.

- Parents and guardians who claim exemptions should be required to revisit the decision annually with a state-approved counselor and should be required to sign a statement each year to renew the exemption.

- Children should be barred from school attendance and other group activities if there is an outbreak of a disease that is preventable by a vaccination from which they have been exempted. Parents and guardians who claim exemptions for their children should acknowledge in writing their understanding that this will occur.

- States that adopt provisions for personal belief exemptions should track exemption rates and periodically reassess the impact that exemptions may have on disease rates.

The Importance of Immunizations

Immunizations are one of the most significant public health interventions in history. Through a progressive, national universal immunization program, four diseases have been eliminated (i.e., endemic disease no longer occurs) from the United States—smallpox (in 1949), polio (1979), measles (2000), and rubella (2004). The occurrence and impact of other infectious diseases have been drastically reduced through vaccination; among these are diphtheria, tetanus, mumps, pertussis (whooping cough), hepatitis A, hepatitis B, varicella (chickenpox), and invasive *Haemophilus influenzae* type b and *Streptococcus pneumoniae*. Hundreds of thousands of deaths have been prevented through routine immunizations and tens of billions of dollars have been saved, making childhood immunizations one of the most cost-effective components of our public health system.

Immunizations are one of the most significant public health interventions in history.

Vaccines protect people from disease in two ways. First, vaccine administration directly imparts immunity to individuals. There are two important caveats, however: a) not all healthy individuals respond optimally to all vaccines, leaving some susceptible to disease despite immunization; and b) not all individuals can be immunized. Children with cancer who are undergoing chemotherapy, for example, either cannot be vaccinated or, if vaccinated, will not respond well. Similarly, young infants are not fully protected until they have completed a series of immunizations. These special groups must therefore rely on a second, indirect mechanism of protection, community immunity—the phenomenon whereby if enough individuals in a community are immunized, diseases cannot spread.

Even a small number of unimmunized individuals in a community can facilitate the spread of disease. In the late 1980s, pockets of unimmunized children in the U.S. led to a resurgence of measles that caused 11,000 hospitalizations and

123 deaths. Unfortunately, the lesson from this experience is still being learned today—2008 saw the largest outbreak of measles in this country in over a decade, an outbreak fueled by purposeful refusal to vaccinate, as opposed to programmatic deficiencies or increased importation of disease from other countries. In other words, recent outbreaks have occurred because individuals who should have been immunized were intentionally not immunized. These outbreaks threaten to return the U.S. to a situation where measles is again endemic.

The Consequences of Vaccine Refusal

Here is an example of what can happen. In January 2008, an unvaccinated 7-year-old boy returned to San Diego with his family from a European trip. He was brought to two doctors' offices with fever, rash, and respiratory symptoms. A few days later he went to a hospital laboratory for tests and later to the emergency room. Because measles was not immediately recognized, no special isolation procedures were used during any of these visits. Over the next few weeks, 11 additional cases of measles occurred in unvaccinated infants and children; these included the index patient's siblings, schoolmates, and children who had also been in the doctors' office at the same time. One of the infants was hospitalized for 2 days and another traveled by airplane while contagious. In total, 70 children who had been exposed to the index case were placed in voluntary home quarantine because their parents either declined measles immunization or they were too young to be vaccinated. This illustrates how diseases can spread because children are unimmunized. It is also important to realize that measles is not a benign condition—complications include pneumonia, encephalitis (brain infection), and death.

The consequences of refusal to vaccinate have played out dramatically in the United Kingdom [U.K.]. In the late 1970s, intense media coverage of anecdotal reports claiming that the pertussis vaccine caused neurological problems (a claim that is false) resulted in a drop in immunization rates from 81% to 31%, resulting in outbreaks of disease that killed hundreds of infants. Similarly, measles was eliminated from the U.K. in 1994. However, in 1998 claims that the MMR (measles, mumps, and rubella) vaccine caused autism (a claim that is false) resulted in a drop in immunization rates to 80–85%, enough to allow, by 2008, the return of endemic measles to the U.K. It is important to emphasize that this happened because many parents refused to have their children immunized.

The ultimate victims ... are the children, who in some cases have lost their lives to diseases that could have been prevented.

Most parents who refuse vaccines for their children do so because they think vaccines may be harmful or that their children are not at risk from vaccine-preventable diseases. Their concerns are fueled by inaccurate reports in the media and on the Internet, celebrity hype, and bad or fraudulent scientific data. Parents are proximate victims of this misinformation— they want to do the right thing for their children, but they believe that the right thing is to avoid vaccination rather than to prevent disease through vaccination. Many of them also believe there are alternative ways to avoid disease, often adhering to practices that have little foundation in empiric science. The ultimate victims, however, are the children, who in some cases have lost their lives to diseases that could have been prevented.

The Need for Vaccine Mandates

Education about vaccine-preventable diseases is not enough to ensure that sufficient numbers of children will be immunized. To a large extent, the success of the U.S. immunization program rests upon state laws and regulations that mandate certain vaccines before entry into child care or school. The ethical basis of these rules is firmly founded in the concepts of *beneficence* (doing the right thing—in this case, protecting individuals and society from the real harm caused by infectious diseases), *nonmaleficence* (not doing harm—vaccines are among the safest and most rigorously evaluated pharmaceuticals used today, and vaccine refusal does harm), and *justice* (equally protecting the rights of all people—in this case, for example, the right of children to be protected despite their parents' beliefs, the right of children who cannot be vaccinated for medical reasons to be protected, and the right of all citizens to benefit from community immunity). While there is a fine line between individual autonomy and the government's interest in protecting its citizens, the courts have consistently upheld the constitutionality of immunization mandates. For all of these reasons, the Task Force on Community Preventive Services, writing some 15 years ago, recommended that vaccination requirements be put in place for childcare, school, and college attendance.

It is wrong to allow parents to exempt their children from required immunizations based on their personal beliefs.

All states allow children who have medical contraindications to vaccination to be exempted from these requirements. Most states also allow for exemption based on religious beliefs, although there is tremendous variability in the rigor with which such beliefs must be proved or documented. In fact, in some states parents simply need to state that "their religion" is against vaccination to be granted an exemption, even though no major religions specifically discourage vaccination.

Exemptions Based on Personal Beliefs

Some states allow for exemption based on the secular personal beliefs of the parents. However, states do not allow religious or personal belief exemption from other laws or regulations designed to protect children. For example, parents cannot be exempted from placing infants in car seats simply because they do not "believe" in them. Likewise, states do not allow exemption from laws designed to protect others. For example, parents cannot allow their children to drive cars without a license, because this may place others (as well as the children) in harm's way. Whether or not children should be vaccinated before childcare or school entry ought not be a matter of "belief". Rather, it should be a matter of public policy based on the best available scientific evidence, and in this case the science is definitive: vaccines are safe and they save lives.

In this context, it is wrong to allow parents to exempt their children from required immunizations based on their personal beliefs. Exemption directly exposes children (who have no personal say in the matter) to harm. For example, the risk of measles among exemptors is 35-fold higher than among vaccinated children, even in communities where over 90% of children are immunized. Likewise, refusal to vaccinate confers upon children a 23-fold higher risk of pertussis and a 9-fold higher risk of chickenpox. Exemptions also confer risk to entire communities. The incidence of pertussis, for example, is 1.5 times higher in states that allow personal belief exemptions than in those that do not. It goes without saying that disease outbreaks are both bad for public health and costly. The state therefore has a vested interest in minimizing the number of children exempted from vaccination, because disease will resurge if too many are exempted, and no one knows *a priori* [beforehand] exactly how many is too many.

The HPV Vaccine Should Be a Part of Mandatory School Vaccines

Ellen M. Daley and Robert J. McDermott

Ellen M. Daley is an associate professor and Robert J. McDermott is a professor in community and family health at the University of South Florida, College of Public Health.

In 1999, the *Morbidity and Mortality Weekly Report (MMWR)* identified the ten most significant public health achievements of the last 100 years. First on the list of accomplishments was vaccination, a biomedical and public health success story responsible for saving millions of lives and preventing untold misery from infectious diseases. Both life expectancy and quality of life have improved because of vaccines that have eradicated diseases such as smallpox, and virtually eliminated childhood diseases such as measles, diphtheria and pertussis (whooping cough).

A particularly good example of the impact of vaccines are ones developed to combat infantile paralysis (polio), first by [researcher Jonas] Salk and later, by [researcher Albert] Sabin. Between 1951 and 1954, immediately prior to the widespread dissemination of Salk's polio vaccine, there were over 16,000 cases of paralytic poliomyelitis, and an average of 1,900 U.S. deaths annually from polio. The Salk vaccine was licensed in the U.S. in 1955, and cases of the disease dropped precipitously to fewer than 1,000 per year until 1962, when the Sabin vaccine was licensed and administered on a widespread basis. By the end of 1962, fewer than 100 cases were seen annually. There has not been a naturally occurring case of polio in the

United States since 1979. Concerted efforts by health and non-profit organizations to disseminate the polio vaccine have reduced the global burden of polio from approximately 350,000 cases per year in the late 1980s to 1,200 cases in 2005, the 50th anniversary of the development of the vaccine.

A Vaccine to Prevent Cancer

A new vaccine has been developed and released for use against a leading cause of death in women worldwide—cervical cancer. The human papillomavirus, or HPV, a species-specific DNA virus with over 100 types identified to date, has been recognized as the causal agent in the development of cervical cancer. It also is associated with other cancers (e.g., anal, penile, vulvar, vaginal, and oral-pharyngeal). Over 30 types of HPV are anogenital, and approximately half of those are oncogeniac [tending to cause cancer]. If left untreated, they have the ability to progress to invasive cancers. Other anogenital HPV types, known as low-risk types, are responsible for genital warts. Whereas genital warts are benign, they are visible and may be a source of embarrassment. HPV is common—a recent U.S. study concluded that overall prevalence among 14–24 year-old women, an age group included in the age range targeted for the HPV vaccine, is 33.8%, and that: "This prevalence corresponds with 7.5 million females with HPV infection, which is higher than the previous estimate of 4.6 million prevalent HPV infections among females in this same age group in the United States." Furthermore, the lifetime likelihood of acquiring HPV is estimated to be 75% or more. Fortunately, infection with HPV also is transient, and in most cases, will clear up through the body's own immune response. According to the National Cancer Institute, about 10% of women have an oncogenic HPV infection at a given time, and they are more common in young women than in older women. Most cervical infections, including ones involving oncogenic types of HPV, clear on their own without causing cancer.

In the U.S., cervical cancer incidence and deaths have significantly decreased because of a well-designed and effective screening program, with an estimated number of 11,150 invasive cervical cancer cases, and 3,670 deaths forecast for 2007. Globally, the picture is grim as more than 250,000 women die annually from cervical cancer, making it the second most common cause of cancer death in women. Moreover, the World Health Organization anticipates a 25% increase in cervical cancer deaths over the next decade if significant interventions do not occur. In addition, 80% of the approximately half million women who will be diagnosed with cervical cancer worldwide live in resource-poor developing countries that do not have the infrastructure to provide cytology screening for the disease. Even in the U.S., the nearly 3,700 women who will die of cervical cancer will have something in common—no screening or no treatment follow-up after screening. These facts speak to access to health care, and the conclusion is clear—cervical cancer is a disease of disparity. Women who are able to afford screening by Pap tests and HPV tests will not likely die of the disease. Rather, the women who lack access to screening and treatment become the victims of an otherwise largely preventable disease and cause of death.

A new vaccine has been developed and released for use against a leading cause of death in women worldwide— cervical cancer.

A Safe and Effective Vaccine

The vaccine, which has passed through three phases of trials to receive licensure and approval from the U.S. Centers for Disease Control and Prevention's Advisory Committee on Immunization Practices (ACIP), has proven to be virtually 100% effective against the two types of HPV (types 16 and 18) responsible for some 70% of all cervical cancers. Both the Merck and the GlaxoSmithKline versions of the HPV vaccines have demonstrated that girls 10 to 15 years of age who received the vaccine prior to exposure to the virus have mounted stronger immune responses than girls and women 16 to 23 years of age in the clinical trials. This finding is one of the reasons that recommendations call for 11–12 year-old girls (possibly as young as age 9) to receive the vaccine at the health care provider's discretion. The vaccine appears to be safe, with only localized injection site reactions noted—an especially important factor in its development, because there is no HPV DNA in the vaccine, only virus-like particles (VLP) that stimulate production of antibodies against the proteins that surround the virus itself.

Mandating school entry immunization against HPV is fundamentally no different than vaccinating youngsters against a wide range of other diseases.

The decision to recommend that girls of ages 11–12 receive the vaccine is sound, based upon the science of the vaccine development, and bolstered by the practicalities of decades of successful vaccination programs. This age group is one that is still accessible as a cohort to receive widespread protection through school entry programs. Implementing the vaccine in this way guarantees that few adolescents will miss out on this protection, and those who do will benefit from herd immunity. Medical and public health professional associations have endorsed the vaccine, including the American College of Obstetrics and Gynecology, the American Academy of Pediatrics, the Society for Adolescent Medicine, and the American Cancer Society.

Opposition to the HPV Vaccine

One might assume that a well-documented, safe, and effective vaccine against the second leading cause of cancer death in women worldwide (the first anti-cancer vaccine of any kind for humans) not only would be hailed as *this* century's greatest public health achievement, but also would be disseminated with lightning speed. Regrettably, such accolade and action cannot be taken for granted. The debate over mandatory school entry vaccination is in full cry nationwide. Whereas some caution is called for in any new achievement that affects the public's health, *this* immunization program, unfortunately, is linked to a sexually transmitted virus. Thus, we propose two questions for readers' consideration: (1) If this vaccine were approved for a virus that was non-genital, or not associated with sexual behavior, would we see delay in its deployment? and (2) If this vaccine combated a virus that caused precancerous and cancerous conditions in boys and men only, would we be confronted with the same level of controversy and reticence about its deployment? There is something fundamentally uncomfortable to Americans who might have to consider that adolescent girls, especially if they are their own daughters, will become sexually active and acquire a sexually transmitted virus. Now is not the time to avoid issues that may be linked to emotions or discomfort. Some women will die of this disease, and at least 70% of those deaths could be prevented through administration of procedures similar to those that have eradicated smallpox and minimized the public health threat of polio and numerous other viral diseases.

Because this virus is transmitted through sexual contact, we are at risk of losing an opportunity to achieve equity in protection against a condition related to poverty and lack of access to care. Vaccinating adolescent girls before they encounter this virus will save thousands, and globally, hundreds of thousands of lives. Mandating school entry immunization against HPV is fundamentally no different than vaccinating youngsters against a wide range of other diseases. Parental consent and "opt out" choices are important, but education about the vaccine is critical for allaying fears. Therefore, health care providers, health educators, and other personnel must reach out to describe the vaccine's safety and effectiveness. If this vaccine is to gain status as the public health achievement of at least the early portion of the current century—we need to move the debate away from antecedent behaviors and advance the vaccine message for preventing unnecessary cancer deaths.

The Flu Vaccine Should Be Mandatory for Health Care Workers

Richard F. Daines

Richard F. Daines was New York State Commissioner of Health until 2010.

As health care workers, we share one of the proudest traditions of all professions: we put our patients' interests ahead of our own.

As a physician who spent more than 20 years working in hospitals, I had the honor of working side by side with other physicians, nurses, food service workers, technicians and transporters in the early and uncertain months of what would become the HIV epidemic, in those first confused days of the anthrax attacks, and when any new international traveler with a fever might have been carrying SARS [severe acute respiratory syndrome]. Never once, no matter what our private fears might have been, did we shirk from our duties or put personal anxieties ahead of the interests of our patients. We took the recommended precautions, worked carefully and cautiously, and gave our patients the compassionate and selfless care for which our professions and institutions are rightly given a special place in our society.

In furtherance of that tradition, on August 13th [2009] the New York State Hospital Review and Planning Council adopted a regulation recommended by the New York State Health Department making approved annual influenza vaccinations mandatory, unless medically contraindicated, for health care workers in hospitals, outpatient clinics and home care services. Legislation applying the same standards to nurs-

Richard F. Daines, "Mandatory Flu Vaccine for Health Care Workers," New York State Department of Health, September 24, 2009. www.health.state.ny.us.

ing home workers has also been proposed. The new regulation will apply first to the routine annual seasonal influenza vaccine now available. With the recent FDA [US Food and Drug Administration] approval of the vaccine for novel H1N1 flu ("swine flu"), the regulation will also apply to that vaccine, just in time for the second wave of novel H1N1 influenza already returning this fall.

The welfare of patients is, without any doubt, best served by the very high rates of staff immunity that can only be achieved with mandatory influenza vaccination.

The Importance of Staff Immunization

Questions about safety and claims of personal preference are understandable. Given the outstanding efficacy and safety record of approved influenza vaccines, our overriding concern then, as health care workers, should be the interests of our patients, not our own sensibilities about mandates. On this, the facts are very clear: the welfare of patients is, without any doubt, best served by the very high rates of staff immunity that can only be achieved with mandatory influenza vaccination—not the 40–50% rates of staff immunization historically achieved with even the most vigorous of voluntary programs. Under voluntary standards, institutional outbreaks occur every flu season. Medical literature convincingly demonstrates that high levels of staff immunity confer protection on those patients who cannot be or have not been effectively vaccinated themselves, while also allowing the institution to remain more fully staffed.

Throughout this fall and winter, more patients than ever may enter our hospitals and clinics without effective influenza immunity. Some will be too young or have other contraindications to vaccination or will have failed to receive vaccinations for a variety of reasons. Others will be too frail for vaccination to be effective. Large numbers of people quite clearly would like to take the new H1N1 vaccine as soon as it is available but will be denied that opportunity because they do not fall into one of the first prioritized groups. For all of these individuals, safety lies in being treated in institutions and by health care personnel with the nearly 100% effective immunity rates seen with other long-mandated vaccinations for health care workers, such as measles and rubella.

In recognition of health care's noble tradition of putting patients' interests first and understanding the need to keep our health care system functioning optimally during this challenge, federal authorities made a remarkable decision regarding the first groups to be given access to the new H1N1 vaccine. In addition to giving highest priority for the new vaccine to those who would receive the direct or personal benefit—pregnant women, caregivers to infants, children and the chronically ill—authorities declared that health care workers would also be given earliest access to the vaccine, ahead of millions of other individuals who have roughly equal or even higher risks of contracting H1N1 influenza with all the discomfort or worse that could mean for them as individuals.

Without mandated vaccinations, many ethically troubling situations may occur.

The Need for Mandatory Vaccination

Knowing that our privileged access to the new vaccine is earned not by our personal risk factors but by the special trust society places in us, then how can we as health care workers maintain that our cooperation in protecting the most vulnerable members of society is nevertheless optional? Without mandated vaccinations, many ethically troubling situations may occur. A health care worker unconcerned about "ordinary flu" might refuse the routine seasonal vaccine, but then expect to be in the front of the line for the "good stuff"—the new and strictly rationed swine flu vaccine. Institutions may find themselves short staffed and less than fully capable if their workers fail to get the seasonal influenza vaccine but then proceed to consume hundreds of doses of the new vaccine, therefore denying those doses to other groups. This scenario will certainly not achieve the staff-wide immunity levels needed to assure patient safety and optimal staffing—the very reasons for which health care workers received their priority in the first place.

Influenza vaccination has saved thousands upon thousands of lives over the last three decades, and thousands more could have been saved if the vaccinations had been more widely used. This year, through effective use of vaccination, we have perhaps the best opportunity to save lives and keep our society and institutions running more smoothly than we have had in 50 years or more. This is not the time for uninformed or self-interested parties to attempt to pump air into long-deflated arguments about vaccine safety in general or to use a single 33-year-old episode to deny decades of safety and saved lives achieved by influenza vaccines prepared in the same way as this year's formulations.

The seasonal influenza vaccine has completed, and before its approval the new H1N1 vaccine also underwent, the most careful development, production and testing processes leading scientists, clinicians and public health authorities can devise. Approval of the H1N1 vaccine was based on the application of the same scientific standards and methods that we believe should govern all our health care practices. We, as health care workers, owe it to our patients and to society in general to demonstrate our confidence in those scientific standards. Even more importantly, we should reconfirm our noble commitment to the tradition of putting patients' interests first by supporting the mandatory influenza vaccination requirement.

Mandatory Vaccinations Are a Violation of Parental Rights

Christopher Klicka

Christopher Klicka was senior counsel for the Home School Legal Defense Association until his death in 2009.

What if, shortly after receiving a routine vaccination, your healthy, 6-month-old baby suddenly came down with a violent fever resulting in brain damage? What if you knew someone whose otherwise normal baby inexplicably died of SIDS (Sudden Infant Death Syndrome) the day after a series of immunizations? Would you vaccinate your children?

On the other hand, what if you heard of a family in your church whose children all contracted whooping cough and were horribly sick for over two months. Night after night, the parents stayed up with their children—holding them while they wheezed and could barely catch their breath. The family was opposed to vaccines on religious grounds and never had their children immunized. Wouldn't you vaccinate your children?

These are true stories. I have encountered scores of such accounts over the last 15 years in my role as senior counsel at the Home School Legal Defense Association [HSLDA].

The Question of Vaccination

Growing scientific and medical evidence demonstrates the dangers of vaccines to some children. Even the federal government concedes there is a problem—it established The National Childhood Vaccine Injury Compensation Program to reimburse parents for children who die from or are permanently disabled by vaccines.

For many years, routine childhood vaccinations have been required in all 50 states. Many states provide religious, medical, or philosophical exemptions for those who need them. But some organizations and individuals argue that across-the-board mandatory immunizations are necessary to protect the health of our nation's youth and to avoid epidemics. These advocates are calling for legislation that would mandate vaccines for all children.

As awareness of the dangers of vaccination grows and the pressure for mandatory immunizations increases, more and more parents are facing the questions: "Should I vaccinate my children?" as well as "Should the government mandate vaccinations for all children?"

Some organizations and individuals argue that across-the-board mandatory immunizations are necessary to protect the health of our nation's youth and to avoid epidemics.

There is no easy answer to the first question. Each family must prayerfully make that decision for their own children.

The answer to the second question is definitely "no." The goal of this article is to explain why mandatory immunizations are troublesome, why existing exemptions to immunization regulations are important, and what your rights as parents are regarding the vaccination of your children.

Harm Caused by Vaccines

Vaccines can sometimes cause permanent injury and death. The National Childhood Vaccine Injury Compensation Program has paid out over $1.5 billion dollars in damages to families for injuries and deaths following a vaccine reaction.

Every year the Food and Drug Administration receives 12,000–14,000 reports to the Vaccine Adverse Events Reporting System (VAERS) of hospitalizations, injuries and deaths following vaccination. This figure does not include the estimated 1 to 10 percent of vaccine injuries that are not reported.

According to the vaccine manufacturers' own product inserts, most vaccines have not been "evaluated or tested for their carcinogenic potential, mutagenic potential, or for impairment of fertility" or "reproductive capacity," and there have been no long-term studies on the cumulative effects on the child's developing immune system of combining all the childhood vaccines together. There are no genetic or lab screening tests available to determine which children will react to a vaccine.

Many parents have strong religious convictions against vaccinating their children.

There is no doubt some vaccines harm some children. No parents can be completely assured that a vaccine administered to their children will be safe. The federal government recognizes these health risks by providing financial remuneration to families whose children have adversely suffered from vaccines. All doctors, before they administer a vaccination to a child, must inform the parents of the potential damaging side effects. Medical science has established that everyone's immune system is different and a baby's immune system is not fully formed until he is almost 3 years old. To administer vaccines in a one-size-fits-all approach poses a significant risk to some individuals.

Take polio, for example. In 1979, the medical community officially declared polio dead. However, ever since then, approximately 10–20 cases of polio are reported each year—all of the cases were contracted by administration of the live polio vaccine.

Religious and Conscientious Objection to Immunizations

Another reason immunizations should not be mandated for all children is that many parents have strong religious convictions against vaccinating their children. Because of the research and case studies demonstrating the risks of vaccination, many parents sincerely believe that such vaccines would harm their children. Generally, these parents believe that children are a gift from God, and that they as parents must fulfill the commands in Scripture regarding raising children. These parents believe that it would be a sin to violate the commands of Scripture. One of those commands is found in Matthew 18:6 where Jesus Christ explains that if they "harm one of these little ones, it is better that a millstone be tied around their neck and they be thrown into the ocean." Since harm could come to their children as a result of vaccines, these parents cannot allow their children to receive immunizations.

As a result of these religious convictions and others, 48 state legislatures have appropriately provided religious or conscientious/philosophical exemptions for parents with similar beliefs. Sixteen states allow for conscientious parental choice exemptions: AZ [Arizona], CA [California], Colorado, Idaho, Louisiana, Maine, Michigan, Minnesota, New Mexico, North Dakota, Ohio, Oklahoma, Utah, Vermont, Washington, and Wisconsin. Only Mississippi and West Virginia have no religious or philosophical exemptions. However, Mississippi does allow an automatic exemption for homeschool students. According to Centers for Disease Control surveys, states allowing for conscientious choice exemptions do not have higher rates of vaccine preventable illnesses.

Arkansas has historically had a religious exemption provision in the state immunization statutes, but on July 25, 2002, a federal court in Arkansas ruled that the exemption was unconstitutional. The court found that the statute unconstitutionally required a person claiming a religious exemption to be an adherent or member of a recognized church or religious denomination whose religious tenants and practices conflicted with the immunization requirement. As written, the law violated the Establishment and Free Exercise Clauses of the First Amendment and the Equal Protection Clause of the Fourteenth Amendment to the United States Constitution. Constitutional principles of religious freedom require that an exemption from the immunization statute be based upon a person's individual religious beliefs, not those of a church or denomination. HSLDA worked with the Arkansas legislature in 2003 to pass a new religious exemption statute that is constitutionally sound.

These religious exemption statutes simply codify the protections of an individual's right to freely exercise their religious belief as guaranteed by the First Amendment of the U.S. Constitution and parallel portions of the state constitutions. These religious exemption statutes have been in place for decades without posing any major risk to public health. Faith-based decisions concerning immunizing one's children have consistently been protected by the courts.

A Parent's Choice

Mounting evidence demonstrates vaccines cause harm to some children. The question is whose children will be harmed? Mandating vaccinations is legislating harm on certain children each year. The decision therefore to vaccinate or not vaccinate a child must be left to the parents and not the state. Homeschool parents especially should have liberty to make this decision because their children are not in constant daily contact with large groups of other children, greatly reducing the likelihood of contracting or spreading disease.

Parents have a fundamental right to direct the education and upbringing of their children, as guaranteed by the Liberty Clause of the Fourteenth Amendment. And the U.S. Supreme Court has recognized this foundational freedom of parental liberty in a long line of cases. Since parental rights are fundamental, the courts must apply a higher standard of review whenever there is a conflict between a parent and the state. The "compelling interest test" requires that a state prove its regulation is essential to fulfill a compelling state interest and is the least restrictive means of fulfilling that interest. The state must also prove this burden with evidence.

The decision . . . to vaccinate or not vaccinate a child must be left to the parents and not the state.

It has long been recognized that the state has a compelling interest in the public health and safety of its citizens. Although immunizations have been shown to be effective in protecting the public health for a majority of citizens, immunizations have also been proven to harm some citizens. There is no conclusive proof, therefore, that mandatory immunizations are essential to protect the public health. Nor is there conclusive evidence that mandatory vaccinations are the least restrictive means to fulfill the state's compelling interest in protecting the public health. The most effective deterrent to these infectious diseases are the enactment and enforcement of public sanitation laws.

In 2000 Iowa's state Senate actually repealed the exemption that allowed a parent to object on religious grounds to the immunization of a child. HSLDA, the Network of Iowa Christian Home Educators, and the National Vaccine Information Center teamed together to fight this bill. By God's grace, the bill was amended in a House committee to reinstate the religious exemption and that battle was won.

Parental liberty is a precious freedom enjoyed by all Americans since the founding of our nation. It is long recognized that, as a general principle, parents act in the best interests of their children and, as a result, make the best decisions for their children. The area of health is no exception. Homeschoolers must work together to keep the decision to immunize in the hands of parents. At HSLDA, we are committed to advancing parental rights as we help homeschool parents who are unduly harassed by social workers and work to keep the religious exemption to immunizations intact.

The HPV Vaccine Should Not Be a Part of Mandatory School Vaccines

Gail Javitt, Deena Berkowitz, and Lawrence O. Gostin

Gail Javitt is a research scholar at Johns Hopkins Berman Institute of Bioethics and adjunct professor at the Georgetown University Law Center. Deena Berkowitz is an assistant professor of pediatrics at George Washington University School of Medicine and Health Services. Lawrence O. Gostin is the Linda D. and Timothy J. O'Neill Professor of Global Health Law at the Georgetown University Law Center.

The human papillomavirus (HPV) is the most common sexually transmitted infection worldwide. In the United States, more than six million people are infected each year. Although most HPV infections are benign, two strains of HPV cause 70 percent of cervical cancer cases. Two other strains of HPV are associated with 90 percent of genital warts cases.

A New Vaccine

In June 2006, the Food and Drug Administration (FDA) approved the first vaccine against HPV. Sold as Gardasil, the quadrivalent vaccine is intended to prevent four strains of HPV associated with cervical cancer, precancerous genital lesions, and genital warts. Following FDA approval, the national Advisory Committee on Immunization Practices (ACIP) recommended routine vaccination for girls ages 11–12 with three doses of quadrivalent HPV vaccine. Thereafter, state legislatures around the country engaged in an intense effort to pass laws mandating vaccination of young girls against HPV. This

Gail Javitt, Deena Berkowitz, and Lawrence O. Gostin, "Assessing Mandatory HPV Vaccination: Who Should Call the Shots?" *Journal of Law, Medicine, and Ethics*, vol. 36, no. 2, Summer 2008, pp. 384, 387–390, 393. Copyright © 2008 by John Wiley & Sons. All rights reserved. Reproduced by permission.

activity was spurred in part by an intense lobbying campaign by Merck, the manufacturer of the vaccine.

The United States has a robust state-based infrastructure for mandatory vaccination that has its roots in the 19th century. Mandating vaccination as a condition for school entry began in the early 1800s and is currently required by all 50 states for several common childhood infectious diseases. Some suggest that mandatory HPV vaccination for minor females fits squarely within this tradition.

Nonetheless, state efforts to mandate HPV vaccination in minors have raised a variety of concerns on legal, ethical, and social grounds. Unlike other diseases for which state legislatures have mandated vaccination for children, HPV is neither transmissible through casual contact nor potentially fatal during childhood. It also would be the first vaccine to be mandated for use exclusively in one gender. As such, HPV vaccine presents a new context for considering vaccine mandates. . . .

State efforts to mandate HPV vaccination in minors have raised a variety of concerns on legal, ethical, and social grounds.

The Limited Data on Adverse Reactions

The approval of a vaccine against cancer-causing HPV strains is a significant public health advance. Particularly in developing countries, which lack the health care resources for routine cervical cancer screening, preventing HPV infection has the potential to save millions of lives. In the face of such a dramatic advance, opposing government-mandated HPV vaccination may seem foolhardy, if not heretical. Yet strong legal, ethical, and policy arguments underlie our position that state-mandated HPV vaccination of minor females is premature.

Although the aim of clinical trials is to generate safety and effectiveness data that can be extrapolated to the general population, it is widely understood that such trials cannot reveal all possible adverse events related to a product. For this reason, post-market adverse event reporting is required for all manufacturers of FDA-approved products, and post-market surveillance (also called "phase IV studies") may be required in certain circumstances. There have been numerous examples in recent years in which unforeseen adverse reactions following product approval led manufacturers to withdraw their product from the market. For example, in August 1998, the FDA approved Rotashield, the first vaccine for the prevention of rotavirus gastroenteritis in infants. About 7,000 children received the vaccine before the FDA granted the manufacturer a license to market the vaccine. Though a few cases of intussusception, or bowel obstruction, were noted during clinical trials, there was no statistical difference between the overall occurrence of intussusception in vaccine compared with placebo recipients. After administration of approximately 1.5 million doses of vaccine, however, 15 cases of intussusception were reported, and were found to be causally related to the vaccine. The manufacturer subsequently withdrew the vaccine from the market in October 1999.

In the case of HPV vaccine, short-term clinical trials in thousands of young women did not reveal serious adverse effects. However, the adverse events reported since the vaccine's approval are, at the very least, a sobering reminder that rare adverse events may surface as the vaccine is administered to millions of girls and young women. Concerns have also been raised that other carcinogenic HPV types not contained in the vaccines will replace HPV types 16 and 18 in the pathological niche.

Questions About Duration of Immunity

The duration of HPV vaccine-induced immunity is unclear. The average follow-up period for Gardasil during clinical trials was 15 months after the third dose of the vaccine. Determining long-term efficacy is complicated by the fact that even during naturally occurring HPV infection, HPV antibodies are not detected in many women. Thus, long-term, follow-up post-licensure studies cannot rely solely upon serologic [reaction of blood serum] measurement of HPV-induced antibody titers [concentrations]. One study indicates that protection against persistent HPV 16 infection remained at 94 percent 3.5 years after vaccination with HPV 16. A second study showed similar protection for types 16 and 18 after 4.5 years.

Questions remain about the vaccine's safety and the duration of its immunity, which call into question the wisdom of mandated vaccination.

The current ACIP recommendation is based on assumptions about duration of immunity and age of sexual debut, among other factors. As the vaccine is used for a longer time period, it may turn out that a different vaccine schedule is more effective. In addition, the effect on co-administration of other vaccines with regard to safety is unknown, as is the vaccines' efficacy with varying dose intervals. Some have also raised concerns about a negative impact of vaccination on cervical cancer screening programs, which are highly effective at reducing cervical cancer mortality. These unknowns must be studied as the vaccine is introduced in the broader population.

At present, therefore, questions remain about the vaccine's safety and the duration of its immunity, which call into question the wisdom of mandated vaccination. Girls receiving the vaccine face some risk of potential adverse events as well as risk that the vaccine will not be completely protective. These risks must be weighed against the state's interest in protecting the public from the harms associated with HPV. As discussed in the next section, the state's interest in protecting the public health does not support mandating HPV vaccination.

The Justification for Mass Immunization

HPV is different in several respects from the vaccines that first led to state-mandated vaccination. Compulsory vaccination laws originated in the early 1800s and were driven by fears of the centuries-old scourge of smallpox and the advent of the vaccine developed by Edward Jenner in 1796. By the 1900s, the vast majority of states had enacted compulsory smallpox vaccination laws. While such laws were not initially tied to school attendance, the coincidental rise of smallpox outbreaks, growth in the number of public schools, and compulsory school attendance laws provided a rationale for compulsory vaccination to prevent the spread of smallpox among school children as well as a means to enforce the requirement by barring unvaccinated children from school. In 1827, Boston became the first city to require all children entering public school to provide evidence of vaccination. Similar laws were enacted by several states during the latter half of the 19th century.

The theory of herd immunity, in which the protective effect of vaccines extends beyond the vaccinated individual to others in the population, is the driving force behind mass immunization programs. Herd immunity theory proposes that, in diseases passed from person to person, it is difficult to maintain a chain of infection when large numbers of a population are immune. With the increase in number of immune individuals present in a population, the lower the likelihood that a susceptible person will come into contact with an infected individual. There is no threshold value above which herd immunity exists, but as vaccination rates increase, indirect protection also increases until the infection is eliminated.

The Supreme Court on Mandatory Vaccination

Courts were soon called on to adjudicate the constitutionality of mandatory vaccination programs. In 1905, the Supreme Court decided the seminal case, *Jacobson v. Massachusetts*, in which it upheld a population-wide smallpox vaccination ordinance challenged by an adult male who refused the vaccine and was fined five dollars. He argued that a compulsory vaccination law was "hostile to the inherent right of every freeman to care for his own body and health in such way as to him seems best." The Court disagreed, adopting a narrower view of individual liberty and emphasizing the duties that citizens have towards each other and to society as a whole. According to the Court, the "liberty secured by the Constitution of the United States . . . does not import an absolute right in each person to be, at all times and in all circumstances, wholly freed from restraint. There are manifold restraints to which every person is necessarily subject for the common good." With respect to compulsory vaccination, the Court stated that "[u]pon the principle of self-defense, of paramount necessity, a community has the right to protect itself against an epidemic of disease which threatens the safety of its members." In the Court's opinion, compulsory vaccination was consistent with a state's traditional police powers, i.e., its power to regulate matters affecting the health, safety, and general welfare of the public.

In reaching its decision, the Court was influenced both by the significant harm posed by smallpox—using the words "epidemic" and "danger" repeatedly—as well as the available scientific evidence demonstrating the efficacy of the vaccine. However, the Court also emphasized that its ruling was applicable only to the case before it, and articulated principles that must be adhered to for such an exercise of police powers to be constitutional. First, there must be a public health necessity. Second, there must be a reasonable relationship between the intervention and public health objective. Third, the intervention may not be arbitrary or oppressive. Finally, the intervention should not pose a health risk to its subject. Thus, while *Jacobson* "stands firmly for the proposition that police powers authorize states to compel vaccination for the public good," it also indicates that "government power must be exercised reasonably to pass constitutional scrutiny." In the 1922 case *Zucht v. King*, the Court reaffirmed its ruling in *Jacobson* in the context of a school-based smallpox vaccination mandate.

The smallpox laws of the 19th century, which were almost without exception upheld by the courts, helped lay the foundation for modern immunization statutes. Many modern-era laws were enacted in response to the transmission of measles in schools in the 1960s and 1970s. In 1977, the federal government launched the Childhood Immunization Initiative, which stressed the importance of strict enforcement of school immunization laws. Currently, all states mandate vaccination as a condition for school entry, and in deciding whether to mandate vaccines, are guided by ACIP recommendations. At present, ACIP recommends vaccination for diphtheria, tetanus, and acellular pertussis (DTaP), Hepatitis B, polio, measles, mumps, and rubella (MMR), varicella (chicken pox), influenza, rotavirus, haemophilus Influenza B (HiB), pneumococcus, Hepatitis A, meningococcus, and, most recently HPV. State mandates differ; for example, whereas all states require DTaP, polio, and measles in order to enter kindergarten, most do not require Hepatitis A.

How the HPV Vaccine Is Different

HPV is different from the vaccines that have previously been mandated by the states. With the exception of tetanus, all of these vaccines fit comfortably within the "public health necessity" principle articulated in *Jacobson* in that the diseases they prevent are highly contagious and are associated with significant morbidity and mortality occurring shortly after exposure. And, while tetanus is not contagious, exposure to *clostridium tetani* is both virtually unavoidable (particularly by children, given their propensity to both play in the dirt and get scratches), life threatening, and fully preventable only through vaccination. Thus, the public health necessity argument plausibly extends to tetanus, albeit for different reasons.

Jacobson's "reasonable relationship" principle is also clearly met by vaccine mandates for the other ACIP recommended vaccines. School-aged children are most at risk while in school because they are more likely to be in close proximity to each other in that setting. All children who attend school are equally at risk of both transmitting and contracting the diseases. Thus, a clear relationship exists between conditioning school attendance on vaccination and the avoidance of the spread of infectious disease within the school environment. Tetanus, a non-contagious disease, is somewhat different, but school-based vaccination can nevertheless be justified in that children will foreseeably be exposed within the school environment (e.g., on the playground) and, if exposed, face a high risk of mortality.

HPV is different from the vaccines that have previously been mandated by the states.

An Insufficient Basis for a Mandate

HPV vaccination, in contrast, does not satisfy these two principles. HPV infection presents no public health necessity, as that term was used in the context of *Jacobson*. While nonsexual transmission routes are theoretically possible, they have not been demonstrated. Like other sexually transmitted diseases which primarily affect adults, it is not immediately life threatening; as such, cervical cancer, if developed, will not manifest for years if not decades. Many women will never be exposed to the cancer-causing strains of HPV; indeed the prevalence of these strains in the U.S. is quite low. Furthermore, many who are exposed will not go on to develop cervical cancer. Thus, conditioning school attendance on HPV vaccination serves only to coerce compliance in the absence of a public health emergency.

The relationship between the government's objective of preventing cervical cancer in women and the means used to achieve it—that is, vaccination of all girls as a condition of school attendance—lacks sufficient rationality. First, given that HPV is transmitted through sexual activity, exposure to HPV is not directly related to school attendance. Second, not all children who attend school are at equal risk of exposure to or transmission of the virus. Those who abstain from sexual conduct are not at risk for transmitting or contracting HPV. Moreover, because HPV screening tests are available, the risk to those who choose to engage in sexual activity is significantly minimized. Because it is questionable how many school-aged children are actually at risk—and for those who are at risk, the risk is not linked to school attendance—there is not a sufficiently rational reason to tie mandatory vaccination to school attendance.

That HPV vaccination may be both medically justified and a prudent public health measure is an insufficient basis for the state to compel children to receive the vaccine.

To be sure, the public health objective that proponents of mandatory HPV vaccination seek to achieve is compelling. Vaccinating girls before sexual debut provides an opportunity to provide protection against an adult onset disease. This opportunity is lost once sexual activity begins and exposure to HPV occurs. However, that HPV vaccination may be both medically justified and a prudent public health measure is an insufficient basis for the state to compel children to receive the vaccine as a condition of school attendance.

Perceived Coercion and Distrust

Childhood vaccination rates in the United States are very high; more than half of the states report meeting the Department of Health and Human Services (HHS) Healthy People 2010 initiative's goal of ≥95 percent vaccination coverage for childhood vaccination. However, from its inception, state mandated vaccination has been accompanied by a small but vocal anti-vaccination movement. Opposition has historically been "fueled by general distrust of government, a rugged sense of individualism, and concerns about the efficacy and safety of vaccines" [as noted by James G. Hodge Jr. and Lawrence O. Gostin]. In recent years, vaccination programs also have been [according to S.P. Calandrillo] a "victim of their tremendous success," as dreaded diseases such as measles and polio have largely disappeared in the United States, taking with them the fear that motivated past generations. Some have noted with alarm the rise in the number of parents opting out of vaccination and of resurgence in anti-vaccination rhetoric making scientifically unsupported allegations that vaccination causes adverse events such as autism.

The rash of state legislation to mandate HPV has led to significant public concern that the government is overreaching its police powers authority. As one conservative columnist [Betsy Hart] has written, "[F]or the government to mandate the expensive vaccine for children would be for Big Brother to reach past the parents and into the home." While some dismiss sentiments such as this one as simply motivated by right wing moral politics, trivializing these concerns is both inappropriate and unwise as a policy matter. Because sexual behavior is involved in transmission, not all children are equally at risk. Thus, it is a reasonable exercise of a parent's judgment to consider his or her child's specific risk and weigh that against the risk of vaccination.

To remove parental autonomy in this case is not warranted and also risks parental rejection of the vaccine because it is perceived as coercive. In contrast, educating the public about the value of the vaccine may be highly effective without risking public backlash. According to one poll, 61 percent of parents with daughters under 18 prefer vaccination, 72 percent would support the inclusion of information about the vaccine in school health classes, and just 45 percent agreed that the vaccine should be included as part of the vaccination routine for all children and adolescents.

Additionally, Merck's aggressive role in lobbying for the passage of state laws mandating HPV has led to some skepticism about whether profit rather than public health has driven the push for state mandates. Even one proponent of state-mandated HPV vaccination acknowledges that Merck "overplayed its hand" by pushing hard for legislation mandating the vaccine. In the face of such criticisms, the company thus ceased its lobbying efforts but indicated it would continue to educate health officials and legislators about the vaccine.

An "opt in" approach to HPV vaccine would not require a change in the existing paradigm and would still likely lead to a high coverage rate.

Opt-Out Provisions

Some argue that liberal opt-out provisions will take care of the coercion and distrust issues. Whether this is true will depend in part on the reasons for which a parent may opt out and the ease of opting out. For example, a parent may not have a religious objection to vaccination in general, but nevertheless may not feel her 11-year-old daughter is at sufficient risk for HPV to warrant vaccination. This sentiment may or may not be captured in a "religious or philosophical" opt-out provision.

Even if opt-out provisions do reduce public distrust issues for HPV, however, liberal opt outs for one vaccine may have a negative impact on other vaccine programs. Currently, with the exception of those who opt out of all vaccines on religious or philosophical grounds, parents must accept all mandated vaccines because no vaccine-by-vaccine selection process exists, which leads to a high rate of vaccine coverage. Switching to an "a la carte" approach, in which parents can consider the risks and benefits of vaccines on a vaccine-by-vaccine basis, would set a dangerous precedent and may lead them to opt out of other vaccines, causing a rise in the transmission of these diseases. In contrast, an "opt in" approach to HPV vaccine would not require a change in the existing paradigm and would still likely lead to a high coverage rate. . . .

Mandating HPV vaccination at the present time would be premature and ill-advised.

No Mandate for the HPV Vaccine

Based on the current scientific evidence, vaccinating girls against HPV before they are sexually active appears to provide significant protection against cervical cancer. The vaccine thus represents a significant public health advance. Nevertheless, mandating HPV vaccination at the present time would be premature and ill-advised. The vaccine is relatively new, and long-term safety and effectiveness in the general population is unknown. Vaccination outcomes of those voluntarily vaccinated should be followed for several years before mandates are imposed. Additionally, the HPV vaccine does not represent a public health necessity of the type that has justified previous vaccine mandates. State mandates could therefore lead to a public backlash that will undermine both HPV vaccination efforts and existing vaccination programs. Finally, the economic consequences of mandating HPV are significant and could have a negative impact on financial support for other vaccines as well as other public health programs. These consequences should be considered before HPV is mandated.

The success of childhood vaccination programs makes them a tempting target for the addition of new vaccines that, while beneficial to public health, exceed the original justifications for the development of such programs and impose new financial burdens on both the government, private physicians, and, ultimately, the public. HPV will not be the last disease that state legislatures will attempt to prevent through mandatory vaccination. Thus, legislatures and public health advocates should consider carefully the consequences of altering the current paradigm for mandatory childhood vaccination and should not mandate HPV vaccination in the absence of a new paradigm to justify such an expansion.

The Flu Vaccine Should Not Be Mandatory for Health Care Workers

David Isaacs and Julie Leask

David Isaacs is a clinical professor of pediatric infectious diseases at the University of Sydney, and Julie Leask is a senior research fellow and manager of social research at the National Centre for Immunisation Research & Surveillance of Vaccine Preventable Diseases at the University of Sydney.

Healthcare workers should be immunised against influenza, for their own protection and to protect their patients against influenza. The issue is whether it is ethical and good practice to make immunisation mandatory.

John Stuart Mill, the British philosopher, famously wrote: "The only purpose for which power can be rightfully exercised over any member of a civilised community, against his will, is to prevent harm to others." This statement of what we now call the principle of autonomy, or a person's right to choose, invalidates any argument that we should force healthcare workers to be immunised for their own sake.

The Justification for Paternalism

The state sometimes exerts benign paternalism to coerce personal choice. Examples are the mandatory use of seat belts or of motorcycle helmets, where the infringement of autonomy is justified by the effect on public health, and where the intervention poses little or no harm to the individual and has been proved to save lives. But it is not clear that this applies to immunisation of healthcare workers. For mandatory immunisation to be acceptable it would have to be effective, not harmful, feasible, and have no alternative.

There is good evidence that patients are vulnerable to nosocomial [acquired in the hospital] influenza. Immunising healthcare workers who care for institutionalised elderly people protects the elderly against influenza and may even prevent deaths, although the benefit is greatest in elderly people who have not been immunised. However, there is virtually no published evidence that immunising healthcare workers protects other patient groups. Immunising carers ought to protect immunocompromised patients who, like elderly people, have an impaired immune response. A literature search, however, found only one observational study in which nosocomial influenza was reduced on a bone marrow transplant unit after a campaign to improve infection control measures and staff immunisation rates. The relative contribution of immunisation could not be elucidated.

Some argue that the severity of influenza in high risk patients, high rates of influenza in healthcare workers, and poor compliance with voluntary programmes are sufficient grounds to make annual immunisation mandatory.

The Potential for Harm

Mandatory immunisation might be justified if it was benign. Although the physical harms from influenza vaccine are generally minor, there are potential psychosocial harms. Mandatory immunisation infringes civil liberty and autonomy. Society commonly recognises the right of people to bodily integrity. Vaccines are invasive, transgressing the traditional boundary of the skin, so there is greater infringement of liberty than from other public health mandates which infringe autonomy, such as helmets or seatbelts. In addition, if those who do not comply face dismissal, this infringes a person's freedom to work and ensure financial security.

Mandatory immunisation may alienate many staff and damage morale. Mandatory immunisation devalues staff by treating them as objects, not people. Furthermore, the message that healthcare workers have to be compelled to be immunised will galvanise and provide ammunition to opponents of immunisation. It risks polarising healthcare workers and producing a backlash with opposite consequences to those intended.

Mandatory influenza immunisation of all healthcare workers is an excessive infringement on autonomy relative to its potential benefits.

The term mandatory implies sanctions for non-compliance. [G.A.] Poland and colleagues [C.L. Ofstead, S.J. Tucker, and T.J. Beebe] argued for religious and medical exemptions with the option of an informed refusal. It could be argued, however, that immunisation is not truly mandatory if you can opt out. We know of two examples of more draconian sanctions.

In 2004, the Virginia Mason Medical Center introduced mandatory influenza immunisation for healthcare workers. The initial penalty for non-compliance was dismissal, but the nurses' union made a successful legal challenge. The hospital agreed to religious or medical exemptions, but unimmunised staff had to wear masks during the influenza season. Immunisation rates rose from 56% to 96%, showing that the policy is feasible. Nevertheless, over 600 nurses protested, and the harm to morale was incalculable.

In 2007, New South Wales Department of Health introduced mandatory immunisation against various infectious diseases (not yet including influenza) for healthcare workers in a wide range of patient care areas. There are no exemptions, and those who do not comply are offered redeployment. The feasibility and acceptability of this policy is untested.

Persuasion Not Coercion

Immunisation of healthcare workers has some parallels with childhood immunisation. We have argued that compulsory childhood immunisation is not justifiable if high levels of immunisation can be achieved without compulsion. Many countries achieve childhood immunisation rates above 95% without mandates, illustrating that well resourced immunisation programmes can succeed. Immunisation is more highly valued by a public persuaded of its benefits, not coerced.

The majority of healthcare workers recognise that influenza immunisation is safe and effective. Can we persuade them to be immunised? Over 75% of nurses were immunised in a programme in British Columbia recently, and convenience was critical for uptake.

We advocate administrative commitment to foster a culture of immunisation in healthcare facilities and stress the need to immunise patients at high risk from influenza. We advocate programmes, using incentives, publicity, ready availability, and feedback to educate healthcare workers about the personal benefit and the benefits to their patients.

Mandatory immunisation would be justifiable only if comprehensive measures to win hearts and minds and to make immunisation part of the organisation's culture were unsuccessful. Even then, mandatory immunisation could be justified only for workers caring for elderly and perhaps immunocompromised patients. We argue that mandatory influenza immunisation of all healthcare workers is an excessive infringement on autonomy relative to its potential benefits.

CHAPTER 4

What Are Some Key Issues Regarding Vaccine Development Worldwide?

Overview: The Future of Vaccines

College of Physicians of Philadelphia

The College of Physicians of Philadelphia is a nonprofit organization that advances the cause of health through such projects as the History of Vaccines, an award-winning educational website.

Vaccines have been a part of the human fight against disease for more than 200 years. The worldwide vaccination campaign eradicated smallpox and immunization has eliminated polio in all but a handful of countries. Childhood vaccination has substantially reduced the morbidity and mortality from infectious diseases in much of the developed world, and yearly influenza vaccination is a commonly accepted practice worldwide to reduce the impact of the seasonal influenza infection.

Future Challenges for Vaccines

While we can attribute many public health successes to vaccination, the future presents continued challenges. Diseases remain for which researchers have been unable to find effective vaccines (such as HIV/AIDS, Malaria, and Leishmaniasis) or that flourish in areas of the world where infrastructures for vaccination are poor or nonexistent and even the currently available vaccines cannot be delivered. In other cases, the cost of vaccines is too high for poorer countries to afford, even though this is often where they are most needed. And, of course, although many of the current vaccines are highly effective, efforts continue to develop vaccines that are more effective than those available today. Thus, researchers continue to explore new possibilities. Higher effectiveness, lower cost, and convenient delivery are some of the main goals.

The first vaccine—the smallpox vaccine—consisted of a live, attenuated virus. "Attenuation" means weakening a virus to the point where it can still provoke an immune response, but doesn't cause illness in a human host.

Many of the vaccines used today, including those for measles and some influenza vaccines, use live, attenuated viruses. Others used killed forms of viruses, pieces of bacteria, or inactivated forms of toxins that the bacteria create. Killed viruses, pieces of bacteria and inactivated toxins can't cause illness, but can still provoke an immune response that protects against future infection.

While we can attribute many public health successes to vaccination, the future presents continued challenges.

New Development Techniques for Vaccines

New techniques are also being employed, however, to create different types of vaccines. Some of these new types include:

- Live recombinant vaccines

- DNA vaccines

Live recombinant vaccines use attenuated viruses (or bacterial strains) as vectors: a virus or bacterium from one disease essentially acts as a delivery device for an immunogenic protein from another infectious agent. In some cases this approach is used to enhance the immune response; in others, it is used when giving the actual agent as a vaccine would cause disease. For example, HIV cannot be attenuated enough to be given as a vaccine in humans—it could cause AIDS.

Starting with a complete virus, researchers identity a section of the virus's DNA that is not necessary for replication. One or more genes that code for immunogens of other pathogens are then inserted into this region. (Each gene essentially contains instructions that tell the body how to make a certain protein. In this case, researchers select genes that code for a protein specific to the target pathogen: an immunogen that will generate an immune response to that pathogen.) For example, a baculovirus (a virus that only infects insects) can be used as a vector and the gene for a particular immunogenic surface protein of an influenza virus may be inserted.

When the modified virus is introduced into a person's body, the immunogen is expressed and presented, generating an immune response against the immunogen—and, as a result, against the pathogen it originates from. In addition to insect viruses, human adenoviruses have been considered as potential vectors for use in recombinant vaccines, particularly against diseases such as AIDS. The vaccinia virus, which is the basis for the smallpox vaccine, was the first used in live recombinant vaccine approaches. Experimental recombinant vaccinia strains have been designed to deliver protection against influenza, rabies, and hepatitis B, among other diseases.

DNA vaccines consist of DNA coding for a particular antigen, which is directly injected into the muscle. The DNA itself inserts into the individual's cells, which then produce the antigen from the infectious agent. Since this antigen is foreign, it generates an immune response. This type of vaccine has the benefit of being relatively easy to produce, since DNA is very stable and easy to manufacture, but is still experimental because no DNA-based vaccines have been shown to elicit the substantial immune response required to prevent infection. Researchers are hopeful, however, that DNA vaccines may be able to generate immunity against parasitic diseases such as malaria—currently, there is no human vaccine in use against a parasite.

New Delivery Techniques for Vaccines

When you think of vaccination, you probably think of a doctor or nurse administering a shot. Future immunization delivery methods, however, may be quite different from what we use today.

Inhaled vaccines, for example, are already used in some cases: influenza vaccines have been made in the form of a nasal spray. One of these vaccines is available every year for seasonal flu. Other possibilities include a patch application, where a patch containing a matrix of extremely tiny needles delivers a vaccine without the use of a syringe. This method of delivery could be particularly useful in remote areas, as its application would not require delivery by a trained medical person, which is generally needed for vaccines delivered as a shot by syringe.

The continuing success of vaccines against so many infectious diseases has inspired scientists to try to use similar methods to combat diseases that remain lethal to many people.

Another issue researchers are attempting to address is the so-called cold chain problem. Many vaccines require cool storage temperatures in order to remain viable. Unfortunately, temperature-controlled storage is often unavailable in parts of the world where vaccination is vital for disease control. One of the reasons smallpox eradication was successful was that the smallpox vaccine could be stored at relatively high temperatures and remain viable for reasonable periods of time; some contemporary vaccines, however, cannot withstand such temperatures. The eruption of the Eyjafjallajokull volcano in Iceland in April 2010 brought air traffic to a standstill in Northern Europe, including planes carrying 15 million doses of polio vaccine bound for West Africa. Officials feared that the delay in delivering the vaccines would allow polio to spread, or that temperatures in the cargo holds of the grounded planes would render the vaccines ineffective.

A New Stabilization Method

Such situations highlight the need for vaccine materials that can be easily transported in a range of conditions and still remain viable. One possible approach to this problem was studied in early 2010 by researchers at the Jenner Institute of the University of Oxford. Starting with a small filter-like membrane, the researchers coated it with an ultrathin layer of sugar glass, with viral particles trapped inside it. In this form, the viruses the researchers used could be stored at temperatures of up to 113°F for six months without losing their ability to provoke an immune response. By comparison, when maintained in liquid storage at 113°F for just one week, one of the two viruses tested was essentially destroyed.

The researchers also demonstrated that the vaccine material could be placed in a holder designed to attach to a syringe, allowing a vaccinator to prepare the vaccine material (with a fluid medium inside the syringe) and administer the vaccine almost simultaneously.

Although this research was preliminary, it offers a promising new avenue for vaccine storage and delivery. With a stabilization method like this one, widespread vaccination campaigns may be possible in areas previously difficult or impossible to reach.

The future of immunization depends on the success of medical research for vaccines that are simpler to administer, will survive transport even without refrigeration, and will provide a more substantial and long-lasting immune response. And in parallel, the continuing success of vaccines against so many infectious diseases has inspired scientists to try to use similar methods to combat diseases that remain lethal to many people, such as malaria, HIV/AIDS, and other diseases for which there are not yet vaccines.

An AIDS Vaccine Is Possible and Must Be a Global Effort

International AIDS Vaccine Initiative (IAVI)

The International AIDS Vaccine Initiative is working to ensure the development of a preventive AIDS vaccine that is safe, effective, and accessible to all people.

Right now, no AIDS vaccine exists, although many possible vaccines are in the development and testing stages. People who are not infected with HIV would use a preventive AIDS vaccine to protect themselves from infection or disease in case of future exposure to the virus.

There will never be a single solution to HIV and AIDS, so any future vaccine will need to be used in conjunction with other prevention and treatment interventions, such as condoms, male circumcision, and antiretroviral therapy. A vaccine will be essential to ending the AIDS pandemic.

An AIDS Vaccine Is Possible

Developing an AIDS vaccine poses challenges that researchers have not encountered to the same degree in the development of other vaccines.

Vaccine development strategies that worked well for other diseases, such as measles, use weakened forms of the virus in the vaccines. This strategy is not used in AIDS vaccine development due to concern that the weakened form could change back into the disease-causing form of HIV. Another challenge is that HIV changes rapidly and can evade immune responses in many people, making it difficult for researchers to study the virus and the human immune response. These represent just a couple of the challenges being faced by AIDS vaccine researchers.

There are sound scientific reasons, however, to believe that a vaccine is possible. Most humans control HIV for many years before developing AIDS. A small number never contract the virus despite repeated exposure. Vaccine studies in non-human primates show that infection can be prevented entirely. Most important, vaccine candidates evaluated in a large clinical trial completed in Thailand in 2009 were found to be 31 percent effective in preventing HIV infection. Though modest, the result established that a vaccine can protect people from HIV. Immunological analysis of samples collected in that trial have shed some light on how the vaccine candidates evaluated in that trial blocked HIV transmission. With such strong evidence in humans and in animals, experts believe a vaccine is possible.

The Challenge of HIV Subtypes

Although the primary goal is to develop a vaccine that can be used worldwide, it is still unknown whether that goal is achievable.

There are different forms of HIV, called subtypes or clades, in different parts of the world. More than nine major subtypes have been identified globally, and there is much variation within each subtype as well.

Currently, no one knows if one vaccine will protect against different subtypes of the virus. Therefore, it is important to test a candidate vaccine in various parts of the world where different subtypes are found.

The Need for a Global Effort

Research must take place in the countries and populations most affected by the global epidemic. This will help determine whether a vaccine will be safe and effective for these populations, and to ensure that an eventual vaccine, once proven safe and effective, can be introduced quickly where it is needed most.

AIDS vaccine research is ongoing in both Western and developing countries. Trials in developing countries are often led by in-country researchers who collaborate with researchers and trial sponsors from other countries. Such partnerships help ensure that research efforts are regionally relevant, and that trials are appropriately conducted and accepted by the surrounding community.

The global AIDS vaccine research effort is not just a scientific pursuit. The active involvement of stakeholders such as policymakers and civil society groups is an integral part of maintaining political, social, and economic commitment to the field at local, national, and global levels.

AIDS Vaccine Trials

All clinical trials, including AIDS vaccine trials, must pass careful review before they receive approval to begin, to make sure that they are scientifically and ethically sound. AIDS vaccine trials follow strict international ethical guidelines and undergo evaluation by local review boards. Review of the trials ensures that each volunteer's well-being and human rights are protected. Examples of volunteer safeguards include confidentiality, the right to leave the trial at any time, and non-coerced, fully informed consent.

When someone is deciding whether or not to participate in a trial, that person must fully understand key information about the trial to make an informed decision about participation. Review of the study by local and national regulatory bodies helps ensure that participants are not unfairly influenced to participate by anyone—friends, family, or trial site staff.

There is no possibility of a volunteer becoming HIV-infected from a trial vaccine because these vaccine candidates do not contain HIV. The vaccine candidates typically contain only copies of pieces of genetic material from HIV. These small molecules are meant to cause the body to create an immune response against HIV, *but they cannot cause HIV infection.*

Everyone should protect himself or herself against HIV and other sexually transmitted infections. People who join a clinical trial should *NOT* count on the trial vaccine to protect them against HIV infection! In fact, the purpose of the research is to find out whether the candidate vaccine works.

When trials begin, researchers do not know for sure how a candidate vaccine might affect a volunteer's risk of HIV infection or disease if exposed through such means as sexual transmission—the level of risk might be less, the same, or more than if the volunteer had not received the experimental vaccine.

Even a partially-effective AIDS vaccine can have a significant impact on the global epidemic if given to a large segment of the population.

Despite efforts to help trial participants reduce their risk of infection, some volunteers may become HIV-infected; these infections are not caused by the candidate vaccine, but occur from exposure to the virus through means such as sexual transmission or injecting drug use. Even though volunteers receive counselling about how to prevent HIV, some people might still take risks or become exposed in other ways. Volunteers who do become infected with HIV through sexual or other exposure have access to medical care as agreed with national and local stakeholders. Anyone who has HIV should receive comprehensive HIV treatment, care, and counselling.

Access to an Eventual AIDS Vaccine

Some key players in the AIDS vaccine field are already addressing access issues for people who will most need the vaccine once it is available. New strategies are being developed to help ensure that vaccines will be affordable, especially in developing countries. This can only happen through partnerships and agreements between many players, including governments, donors, international organisations, and the private sector.

Providing clear and accurate information about AIDS vaccines will be especially important once they are available. Initial AIDS vaccines will most likely be partially effective, meaning they will not prevent HIV infection in every vaccine recipient. It will be very important for people to understand that receiving a vaccine does not guarantee prevention of infection so that they continue to practice other HIV prevention methods. Public health efforts to encourage use of prevention methods such as condoms and clean needles must continue at the time of vaccine introduction.

Even a partially-effective AIDS vaccine can have a significant impact on the global epidemic if given to a large segment of the population. Access for affected populations should be at the forefront of AIDS vaccine introduction efforts.

More Money Is Needed for Vaccines for Pandemic Flu

Gary S. Becker

Gary S. Becker is the Rose-Marie and Jack R. Anderson Senior Fellow at the Hoover Institution and a professor of economic, sociology, and business at the University of Chicago.

Every century or so, a major flu pandemic (an epidemic with a global impact) strikes. The last one, the great pandemic of 1918–20, infected many hundreds of millions of people and killed 50 million to 100 million men and women around the world. The Asian flu of 1957 is estimated to have killed 2 million people, and the pandemic of 1968 killed more than 1 million. Various false alarms also have occurred, such as the swine flu outbreak in 1976 in the United States, where more than 40 million people received flu vaccinations, thirty people died from the vaccinations, and few died from the flu itself. This year's [2009] swine flu cases raised fears of the next "big one" before the flu settled down to an apparently manageable, though widespread, outbreak. What would be the economic cost of a global pandemic today?

The Cost of a Flu Pandemic

As of midsummer, about 95,000 people worldwide had confirmed cases of swine flu, with 425 deaths reported. Even as the flu season shifted to the Southern Hemisphere and the illness seemed to be no more dangerous than the common flu, health officials advised caution because flu pandemics, including the great pandemic, often go through phases in which the first spread is rather moderate and the next waves are much more devastating. Whatever the course of this particular outbreak, health officials are confident that before long a major pandemic will strike that could wreak devastation throughout the world.

Note that flu pandemics involve a huge externality because infected individuals have limited incentives to take into consideration the likelihood of infecting others when deciding how much contact to have with other people. This externality justifies a significant public health involvement in trying to control the spread of flu during a pandemic.

Consider the cost of a modern flu pandemic as devastating as the great pandemic. Fifty million deaths in 1918–20 constituted about 2.8 percent of the world population at that time. Because population has grown twofold since then, a flu pandemic today that killed 2.8 percent of all people would take a staggering 150 million lives. That number can be converted into an equally staggering monetary value through findings on what people are willing to pay to avoid fatal health and other risks—what economists call the statistical value of life. It is estimated that this statistical value of life for a typical young adult in the United States is about $5 million.

Health officials are confident that before long a major pandemic will strike that could wreak devastation throughout the world.

The Next Pandemic

To calculate the aggregate cost of another such great pandemic, we assume that the comparable statistical values of life in other countries equal $5 million times the ratio of the per capita incomes to the U.S. per capita income. For example, the statistical value of life for a typical young person in a country with half the per capita income of the United States would be $2.5 million. Then if we assume that the same percent of the population would die from such a pandemic in all countries, the total cost of a pandemic equal in severity to the great pandemic would be more than $100 trillion. This huge amount dwarfs the effects of such a pandemic on world GDP [gross domestic product], the economic impact that is usually calculated.

A *Lancet* study published in December 2006 estimated that a modern pandemic of equal virulence to the Spanish flu that caused the great pandemic would kill not 150 million people but about 60 million. It also claims that these deaths would be very much concentrated in poorer countries. Using the authors' calculations to adjust my estimate of what people of the world would be willing to pay to avoid such a pandemic would reduce the estimated total cost to about $20 trillion.

Vaccines might be produced quickly enough to inoculate huge numbers against new flu strains, even highly virulent ones.

Important developments in the world health care system might reduce even further the number of deaths from a virulent flu outbreak today. It's true that the explosion in world population since 1919, the growth of cities at the expense of the countryside, and the development of air travel have led to much greater movement across national boundaries, which implies that the spread of flu has become a lot easier. But it's also a lot easier to contain the spread and severity of a flu pandemic. Public health officials can isolate and identify the genetic composition of flu strains much more quickly than during the great pandemic. Officials of different countries are also in much greater contact with each other and can collaborate to partly quarantine victims of future pandemics.

The Need for More Spending

Perhaps the most important lifesaving developments in recent decades are vaccines and antiviral drugs such as Tamiflu. Vaccines might be produced quickly enough to inoculate huge numbers against new flu strains, even highly virulent ones. When taken early enough, the antivirals can greatly moderate the course of an illness and speed recovery. The United States and the European Union apparently have large enough stocks of antivirals to treat about 16 percent of their populations— the U.S. supply covers about 50 million people; Japan has even larger drug supplies relative to its population. The poorer countries of Africa and elsewhere are the least prepared to fight a major pandemic.

Of course, new flu strains may emerge that cannot be treated by the known antivirals (the first cases of Tamiflu-resistant swine flu appeared in the middle of last summer). And bioterrorists may be able to produce and spread highly deadly viruses of all kinds. At the same time, drug companies are better prepared than even a few years ago to ramp up production of old drugs and to develop additional drugs to fight new flu strains and other viruses not treatable by present drugs.

I have indicated elsewhere that the vast majority of people are willing to pay a lot to gain protection against deadly flu viruses, which is why it would be desirable to greatly increase the stockpile of drugs and vaccines even if the probability of another pandemic were low and its nature unknown. For example, the expected worldwide cost in terms of willingness to pay to avoid the risk of another great pandemic that had a 1-in-100 probability of occurring during the next twenty years would be approximately one one-hundredth times $20 trillion, or about $200 billion. This cost would justify sizable increases in world spending on antiviral drug and flu vaccines.

Decisions About How to Combat Pandemic Flu Need to Be Restrained

Henry I. Miller

Henry I. Miller is the Robert Wesson Fellow in Scientific Philosophy and Public Policy at the Hoover Institution.

NOW that the H1N1 swine-flu outbreak appears to be waning, it's time to draw important lessons from what happened.

First, the pronouncements from the World Health Organization [WHO], a United Nations agency, were disappointing. Most flu and public-health experts consider the WHO's decision last week [April 29, 2009] to raise the pandemic flu threat to Level 5, "Pandemic Imminent," to have been alarmist and unwarranted.

The "imminence" of a pandemic pushed governments and individuals into unwise, drastic decisions: unnecessary school, business and event closings and purchases of anti-flu drugs on the Internet (as often as not, a source of counterfeits). Many media images showed people wearing the wrong kinds of masks: Those with pores small enough to filter out flu virus are "N95 respirators," used for working around fiberglass or wood dust.

But flawed decision-making is typical of the WHO, a scientifically mediocre, unaccountable and self-serving organization whose leadership is based on a kind of international affirmative action instead of merit. The WHO may be well-equipped to perform and report worldwide surveillance, but its policy role should be limited.

Second, the media were for the most part unhelpful. Applying the ethic "if it bleeds, it leads," they hyped the story breathlessly, omitting necessary context. Largely ignored was the realization that yet another flu virus—the garden-variety "seasonal flu"—is a consistent, big-time killer year in, year out.

Even if we did begin to formulate and manufacture vaccine immediately, it would arrive far too late to attenuate the first wave of infections.

Vaccines and Other Precautions

That fact must be remembered when we need to make real-time decisions about how to respond to such outbreaks—about whether to start a crash program to make vaccine from the new virus, for example.

The decisions to be made are difficult. Should countries close their borders and restrict domestic and international trade? Should they rush to prepare vast amounts of vaccine? What should be the criteria for prophylaxis or treatment with anti-flu drugs?

The border closings would deny access to many items made abroad that are needed during a pandemic, including masks and gloves, electrical circuits for ventilators and certain pharmaceuticals.

Worst of all, the WHO made a huge misstep in putting vaccine companies on notice that it was likely to request that some commercial-flu-vaccine production be directed at H1N1 swine flu. Even if we did begin to formulate and manufacture vaccine immediately, it would arrive far too late to attenuate the first wave of infections.

It's true that a crash vaccine-manufacturing program could blunt a second flu wave, if there is one. (Historically, flu pandemics have come in two or three waves, lasting 13 to 23 months.) But such a swine-flu vaccine would necessarily be made at the expense of next winter's vaccine for seasonal flu—which kills 30,000 to 40,000 a year on average in America (and many more worldwide), *even when a significant fraction of the population is immunized with an effective vaccine.* Thus, the absence of adequate vaccine supplies for next winter's seasonal flu would invite a public-health catastrophe.

Public Health Decisions

Although pandemic strains of flu often are much worse than the seasonal-flu viruses, the H1N1 virus causing the current outbreak seems to be relatively benign. Except for in Mexico, illnesses have generally been mild, hospitalizations few and mortality minimal.

What do we know, then, two weeks after the outbreak? For one thing, we're bedeviled by cost-benefit decisions. Only hindsight will pick the winners and losers, but it appears that US public-health officials—especially those at the Centers for Disease Control and the National Institutes of Health, and also those in New York City—have acted with appropriate judgment and restraint.

Federal officials have accumulated, analyzed and disseminated information, offering advice to the public and to health professionals. They're preparing for a worsening of the situation but aren't overreacting. They've made testing kits widely available around the country and abroad. Their laboratories are working around the clock, performing sequencing and other analyses of swine-flu isolates, and they're preparing contingency plans should the situation change suddenly.

Perhaps most important, they aren't making dubious, alarmist pronouncements.

The ease of international travel raises the stakes for the prospect of emerging diseases. The swine-flu outbreak could serve as a valuable wake-up call, making us think critically about who'll be entrusted with public-health decisions.

Organizations to Contact

The editors have compiled the following list of organizations concerned with the issues debated in this book. The descriptions are derived from materials provided by the organizations. All have publications or information available for interested readers. The list was compiled on the date of publication of the present volume; the information presented here may change. Be aware that many organizations take several weeks or longer to respond to inquiries, so allow as much time as possible.

Centers for Disease Control and Prevention (CDC)
1600 Clifton Rd., Atlanta, GA   30333
(800) 232-4636
e-mail: cdcinfo@cdc.gov
website: www.cdc.gov

The Centers for Disease Control and Prevention, a part of the US Department of Health and Human Services, is the primary federal agency for conducting and supporting public health activities in the United States. Through research and education, the CDC is dedicated to protecting health and promoting quality of life through the prevention and control of disease, injury, and disability. Among the many publications available at the agency's website regarding vaccines and immunizations are childhood, adolescent, and adult immunization schedules; information about reasons to vaccinate and the importance of vaccinating; and vaccine safety reports, including access to the Vaccine Adverse Event Reporting System (VAERS).

Immunization Action Coalition (IAC)
1573 Selby Ave., Suite 234, St. Paul, MN   55104
(651) 647-9009 • fax: (651) 647-9131
e-mail: admin@immunize.org
website: www.immunize.org

The Immunization Action Coalition works to increase immunization rates and prevent disease. The IAC creates educational materials and facilitates communication about the safety, efficacy, and use of vaccines within the broad immunization community of patients, parents, health care organizations, and government health agencies. The organization publishes numerous reports and vaccination schedules, including the brochure "What If You Don't Immunize Your Child?"

Institute for Vaccine Safety (IVS)
Johns Hopkins Bloomberg School of Public Health
615 N Wolfe St., Room W5041, Baltimore, MD   21205
(410) 955-2955 • fax: (410) 502-6733
e-mail: info@hopkinsvaccine.org
website: www.vaccinesafety.edu

The Institute for Vaccine Safety is an organization within the Johns Hopkins Bloomberg School of Public Health that works to obtain and disseminate objective information on the safety of recommended immunizations. IVS provides a forum for dissemination of data regarding specific issues concerning the safety of immunizations, investigates safety questions, and conducts research. The organization sponsors academic publications, provides information about state school vaccination law exemptions, and provides information on vaccine legislation.

International AIDS Vaccine Initiative (IAVI)
110 William St., Floor 27, New York, NY   10038-3901
(212) 847-1111
website: www.iavi.org

IAVI is a nonprofit product development partnership working to ensure the development of preventive AIDS vaccines. IAVI invests the bulk of its resources in the research and clinical assessment of candidate vaccines against strains of HIV that are prevalent in the developing world, where some 95 percent of new HIV infections occur. The organization publishes *VAX* and the *IAVI Report*, and several other publications are available at its website.

National Network for Immunization Information (NNii)

301 University Blvd., Galveston, TX   77555-0350
(409) 772-0199 • fax: (409) 772-5208
e-mail: nnii@i4ph.org
website: www.immunizationinfo.org

The National Network for Immunization Information has established affiliations with the Infectious Diseases Society of America, the Pediatric Infectious Diseases Society, the American Academy of Pediatrics, the American Nurses Association, the American Academy of Family Physicians, the National Association of Pediatric Nurse Practitioners, the American College of Obstetricians and Gynecologists, the University of Texas Medical Branch, the Society for Adolescent Medicine, and the American Medical Association. NNii provides the public, health professionals, policymakers, and the media with up-to-date information related to immunization to help them understand the issues and make informed decisions. NNii publishes numerous briefs, papers, and pamphlets, including "Do Multiple Vaccines Overwhelm the Immune System?" available on its website.

National Vaccine Information Center (NVIC)

407 Church St., Suite H, Vienna, VA   22180
(703) 938-0342 • fax: (703) 938-5768
e-mail: contactNVIC@gmail.com
website: www.nvic.org

The National Vaccine Information Center is dedicated to defending the right to informed consent to medical interventions, and to preventing vaccine injuries and deaths through public education. NVIC provides assistance to those who have suffered vaccine reactions; promotes research to evaluate vaccine safety and effectiveness; and monitors vaccine research, development, regulation, policymaking, and legislation. Many resources are available at the organization's website, including position papers and articles, including "Promoting Vaccination, Fear, Hate, and Discrimination."

ThinkTwice Global Vaccine Institute
PO Box 9638, Santa Fe, NM 87504
(505) 983-1856
e-mail: global@thinktwice.com
website: www.thinktwice.com

The ThinkTwice Global Vaccine Institute was established in 1996 to provide parents and other concerned people with educational resources enabling them to make more informed vaccine decisions. ThinkTwice encourages an uncensored exchange of vaccine information and supports every family's right to accept or reject vaccines. The institute has studies, articles, and books available at its website, including the book *Vaccine Safety Manual for Concerned Families and Health Practitioners.*

Vaccination Liberation
PO Box 457, Spirit Lake, ID 83869-0457
(888) 249-1421
e-mail: ingri29@vaclib.com
website: www.vaclib.org

Vaccination Liberation is part of a national grassroots network dedicated to providing information on vaccinations not often made available to the public so that people can avoid and refuse vaccines. Vaccination Liberation works to dispute claims that vaccines are necessary, safe, and effective; expand awareness of alternatives in healthcare; preserve the right to abstain from vaccination; and repeal all compulsory vaccination laws nationwide. The organization has abundant information available at its website, including the article "How to Legally Avoid School Immunizations."

Vaccine Education Center
The Children's Hospital of Philadelphia
34th St. and Civic Center Blvd., Philadelphia, PA 19104
(215) 590-1000
website: www.vaccine.chop.edu

The Vaccine Education Center at the Children's Hospital of Philadelphia educates parents and health care providers about vaccines and immunizations. The Vaccine Education Center provides videos, informational tear sheets, and information on every vaccine. Among the numerous publications available for download from the Center's website is "Too Many Vaccines? What You Should Know."

VaccineEthics.org
University of Pennsylvania Center for Bioethics
3401 Market St., Suite 320, Philadelphia, PA   19104
(215) 898-7136
website: www.vaccineethics.org

VaccineEthics.org is a production of the University of Pennsylvania Center for Bioethics, which offers information on ethical issues associated with vaccines and vaccination programs. The center has identified and studied ethical challenges present throughout the vaccine life-cycle; organized regional, national, and international meetings; and contributed to the scholarly and public dialogues on vaccine ethics and policy. Available at its website are issue briefs such as "Informed Consent in Vaccination."

Bibliography

Books

Arthur Allen · *Vaccine: The Controversial Story of Medicine's Greatest Lifesaver.* New York: W.W. Norton, 2008.

James Colgrove · *State of Immunity: The Politics of Vaccination in Twentieth-Century America.* Berkeley, CA: University of California Press, 2006.

Harris L. Coulter and Barbara Loe Fisher · *A Shot in the Dark: Why the P in the DPT Vaccination May Be Hazardous to Your Child's Health.* Garden City, NY: Avery, 1991.

Madelon Lubin Finkel · *Truth, Lies, and Public Health: How We Are Affected When Science and Politics Collide.* Westport, CT: Praeger, 2007.

Barbara Loe Fisher · *The Consumer's Guide to Childhood Vaccines.* Vienna, VA: National Vaccine Information Center, 1997.

Robert Goldberg · *Tabloid Medicine: How the Internet Is Being Used to Hijack Medical Science for Fear and Profit.* New York: Kaplan, 2010.

Louise Kuo Habakus and Mary Holland · *Vaccine Epidemic: How Corporate Greed, Biased Science, and Coercive Government Threaten Our Human Rights, Our Health, and Our Children.* New York: Skyhorse, 2011.

David Kirby — *Evidence of Harm: Mercury in Vaccines and the Autism Epidemic, a Medical Controversy.* New York: St. Martin's Griffin, 2006.

Kurt Link — *The Vaccine Controversy: The History, Use, and Safety of Vaccinations.* Westport, CT: Praeger, 2005.

Gary Marshall — *The Vaccine Handbook.* Ann Arbor, MI: Professional Communications, Inc., 2008.

Neil Z. Miller — *Vaccines: Are They Really Safe and Effective?* Santa Fe, NM: New Atlantean Press, 2008.

Seth Mnookin — *The Panic Virus: A True Story of Medicine, Science, and Fear.* New York: Simon & Schuster, 2011.

Martin Myers and Diego Pineda — *Do Vaccines Cause That?! A Guide for Evaluating Vaccine Safety Concerns.* Galveston, TX: Immunizations for Public Health, 2008.

Paul A. Offit — *Vaccinated: One Man's Quest to Defeat the World's Deadliest Diseases.* New York: HarperCollins, 2008.

Paul A. Offit — *Deadly Choices: How the Anti-Vaccine Movement Threatens Us All.* New York: Basic Books, 2011.

Robert Sears — *The Vaccine Book: Making the Right Decision for Your Child.* New York: Little, Brown, 2007.

Sherri J.
Tenpenny

Saying No to Vaccines. Middleburg
Heights, OH: NMA Media-Press,
2008.

Andrew J.
Wakefield

*Callous Disregard: Autism and
Vaccine—The Truth Behind a Tragedy.*
New York: Skyhorse Publishing, 2010.

Stanley
Williamson

*The Vaccination Controversy: The
Rise, Reign, and Fall of Compulsory
Vaccination for Smallpox.* Liverpool,
UK: Liverpool University Press, 2008.

Periodicals and Internet Sources

Jill U. Adams

"Contagious Disease's Spread
Highlights Dilemma over
Unvaccinated Kids," *Los Angeles
Times*, February 23, 2009.

Arthur Allen

"Immune to Reason: Are Vaccine
Skeptics Putting Your Kids at Risk?"
Mother Jones, September/October
2008.

John M. Barry

"Invest in Vaccines to Avert
Pandemic," *Atlanta
Journal-Constitution*, July 1, 2009.

Alicia M. Bell

"Hold the Hype on HPV," *Women's
Health Activist*, May–June 2007.

Seth Berkley

"Have Faith in an AIDS Vaccine,"
New York Times, October 19, 2009.

Sandra G.
Boodman

"Faith Lets Some Kids Skip Shots,"
Washington Post, June 10, 2008.

Mary Carmichael   "The Search for Solutions," *Newsweek*, October 1, 2007.

Frances Childs   "How the Middle-Class MMR Refuseniks Are Putting Every Child at Risk," *Mail Online*, February 19, 2009. www.dailymail.co.uk.

College of Physicians of Philadelphia   "Vaccine Development, Testing, and Regulation," History of Vaccines, 2011. www.historyofvaccines.org.

Ryan Coller   "The Autism/Vaccine Myth," *Los Angeles Times*, May 3, 2009.

Committee on Infectious Diseases   "Policy Statement Recommendation for Mandatory Influenza Immunization of All Health Care Personnel," *Pediatrics*, October 2010.

Theodore Dalrymple   "The World Before Vaccine Is Too Easy to Forget," *Times* (London), September 30, 2009.

Leslie Donald   "A Nose Rinse Might Be as Good as a Flu Shot," *Record* (Kitchener, Ontario), November 13, 2009.

Gary L. Freed, Sarah J. Clark, Amy T. Butchart, Dianne C. Singer, and Matthew M. Davis   "Parental Vaccine Safety Concerns in 2009," *Pediatrics*, April 2010.

Michael Fullerton   "Swine Flu Madness," OpEdNews .com, November 4, 2009. www.oped news.com.

John Gapper   "The Hidden Cost of Free Vaccines," *Financial Times*, June 18, 2009.

Laurie Garrett and Dana March   "The Long-Term Evidence for Vaccines," *Newsweek*, December 7, 2009.

Juliet Guichon and Ian Mitchell   "Refusing to Get Vaccinated Is Selfish," *Globe & Mail*, October 27, 2009.

Eben Harrell   "Do Flu Vaccines Really Work? A Skeptic's View," *Time*, February 27, 2010.

Connor Henderson   "Risks of H1N1 Vaccine Have Been Exaggerated," *Record* (Kitchener, Ontario), December 30, 2009.

Claudia Kalb   "Stomping Through a Medical Minefield," *Newsweek*, October 25, 2008.

Homayoon Khanlou and Michael Weinstein   "No Results? No Research Money," *Los Angeles Times*, April 25, 2008.

Mike King   "Vaccinations' Benefits Proved; Enforce the Law," *Atlanta Journal-Constitution*, October 29, 2008.

Sabra L. Klein and Phyllis Greenberger   "Do Women Need Such Big Flu Shots?" *New York Times*, October 28, 2009.

Shana Kluck   "Mandatory Vaccines Override Parental Rights," United Liberty, October 18, 2008. www.united liberty.org.

Maura Lerner   "Health Employers Giving Flu Vaccine a Shot in the Arm," *Star Tribune*, September 29, 2008.

Megan McArdle   "The Poking Cure," *Atlantic Online*, March 28, 2008. www.theatlantic .com.

Henry I. Miller   "Better Vaccines for the Next Pandemic; New Technologies Promise an End to Shortages," *Washington Times*, December 7, 2009.

Neil Z. Miller   "Overdosed Babies: Are Multiple Vaccines Safe?" ThinkTwice Global Vaccine Institute, 2010. www.think twice.com.

Deroy Murdock   "Let America Have the Smallpox and Anthrax Vaccines," *Human Events*, November 28, 2009.

Alex Newman   "Millions of Expired Swine-Flu Vaccines to Be Destroyed as Criticism Mounts," *New American*, July 2, 2010.

Paul A. Offitt   "Nothing to Fear but the Flu Itself," *New York Times*, October 12, 2009.

Peggy O'Mara   "The Assault on Freedom of Conscience," *Mothering*, March/April 2009.

Glenn Harlan Reynolds
"As Diseases Make Comeback, Why Aren't All Kids Vaccinated?" *Popular Mechanics*, August 1, 2008.

Phyllis Schlafly
"Universal Child Care Poses Threat to Parental Rights," *Human Events*, January 14, 2008.

Michael Wagnitz
"Decision Raises Question: What Exactly Is Thimerosal?" *Capital Times* (Madison, WI), April 18, 2010.

Amy Wallace
"An Epidemic of Fear: How Panicked Parents Skipping Shots Endangers Us All," *Wired*, November 2009.

Grant Warkentin
"Vaccine Conspiracy Bad Science Fiction," *Campbell River Mirror* (Campbell River, British Columbia), November 5, 2009.

Margaret Wente
"Autism, Vaccines, and Fear," *Globe & Mail*, February 4, 2010.

Index

A

Adverse events, 53, 55, 76, 79, 83, 122–123, 129–130
   See also Risks of vaccination
Advisory Committee on Immunization Practices (ACIP), 46, 113, 128, 131, 134
Africa, smallpox and AIDS in, 48–49
AIDS/HIV, 48–49, 148, 151–155
Alternate disease prevention measures, 67–68
American Academy of Pediatrics, 52, 88, 98, 114
American Cancer Society, 114
American College of Obstetrics and Gynecology, 114
American Indians, 37
Amish, 96
Antibodies
   defined, 21
   vaccine efficacy and, 44, 56, 131
Antigen-presenting cells, 21
Antigens, 20–21, 148
Anti-vaccination movement, 137
Antiviral drugs
   efficacy, 66–67
   as preventive measure, 68, 158–159
   stockpiling of, 58–59
Arkansas, exemptions to mandatory vaccination in, 124
Artificially acquired immunity, 24–25

Asian flu of 1957, 60, 61, 156
Asthma, 92
Attenuated viruses, 147–148
Australia, mandatory vaccination in, 143
Autism
   belief in MMR vaccine as cause of, 51, 71
   non-causality of vaccines, 79, 83–87
   temporal association of vaccination and, 52–53
Autonomy (personal), 141–142, 144

B

B Cells, 20–21
Bacteria, 25–26
Bacterial fragments, 99
Beebe, T.J., 143
Beliefs (personal/religious) and vaccination exemption, 104–105, 109–110, 124–125
Bioterrorism, 159
BMJ (formerly *British Medical Journal*), 85–86
Booster vaccines, 44, 91–92, 94, 97
Bordetella pertussis, 27
Bowel obstruction, 130

C

Calandrillo, S.P., 137
Cancer
   cervical cancer and HPV, 112–113, 128, 131, 136

vaccine contamination and, 98–99

Carbone, Michele, 99

Centers for Disease Control (CDC)
  disease statistics, 36, 40
  flu vaccination program, 42, 45, 60, 66
  HPV vaccine approval, 113
  swine flu of 1976 response, 46–47
  swine flu of 2009 and, 41, 58, 162
  on temporal association of adverse events and vaccination, 53
  vaccination recommendations, 73, 88, 97, 102

Cervical cancer, 112–113, 128, 131, 136

Cetron, Marty, 41

Chickenpox, 34–35, 56, 93, 94, 110

Childhood Immunization Initiative, 134

Children
  vaccine schedule, 73, 88
  vaccines and asthma, 92
  vaccines and autism, 52–53, 79, 83–87
  See also Infants; Mandatory vaccination; Parents; School entry and mandatory vaccination

China, 99–100

Classen, Bart, 44–45

Clinical trials
  AIDS vaccine, 152, 153–154
  in developing countries, 153
  flu vaccines, 42, 66–67
  HPV vaccine, 113–114, 129–131

placebo-controlled studies, 54–55

Clostridium tetani, 134
  See also Tetanus vaccine

Cochrane Collaboration, 63

Cold chain problem, 149

Colleges and universities, vaccines required by, 94–95

Community immunity, 25–26, 77, 80–81, 87, 95–96, 106–107, 118, 132

Comvax vaccine, 55

Congenital rubella syndrome (CRS), 34

Constitution, US, 124–125

Cox, Nancy, 66

Cytomegalovirus, 94

D

Deadly Choices: How the Anti-Vaccine Movement Threatens Us All (Offit), 74

Death rates
  diphtheria, 36
  influenza and influenza-like illness, 40, 45, 62–63, 64, 65–66, 91, 142, 144
  pertussis, 89
  polio, 89
  from vaccine-related illness, 46

Deer, Brian, 84–86

Delivery techniques, 148–149

Department of Health and Human Services, 136–137

Developing countries
  access to health care in, 113, 154–155
  AIDS vaccine research in, 152–153

cervical cancer and HPV, 113, 129

diseases lacking vaccines in, 146

measles, 31

rubella, 34

Diabetes, vaccination-caused, 44

Diphtheria, 23, 36–37, 48

Disease. *See* Infectious disease

DNA vaccines, 148

Dogmas, medical, 51–53, 57

DTaP vaccine, 32, 92, 134

E

Eddy, Bernice, 99

The elderly

diptheria-related deaths, 36

exposure to vaccinated children, 94

flu-related deaths, 45, 62–63, 64, 65–66, 91, 142, 144

live virus vaccines and, 94

measles virus in, 93

Encephalitis, 30, 39, 107

Enders, John, 52

Epidemics

diphtheria, 37

pertussis, 25, 32–33

polio, 29

preparation for, 41

rubella, 34

smallpox, 47

vaccination as cause of, 47–49

See also Pandemics

Equal Protection Clause, US Constitution, 125

Eradication of infectious disease, 14–16, 27, 29–30, 82, 106, 111, 146, 149

Establishment Clause, US Constitution, 125

Exemptions to mandatory vaccination. *See* Mandatory vaccination exemptions

F

Face masks, 143, 160, 161

Failure of vaccines, 48, 96–97

Fauci, Anthony, 66

FDA (Food and Drug Administration), 60, 86, 118, 122–123, 128, 130

Fever, 22, 121

First Amendment (US Constitution), 125

Fisher, Barbara Loe, 74

Flexnor, Simon, 51

Flu. *See* Influenza and influenza-like illness

Food and Drug Administration (FDA), 60, 86, 118, 122–123, 128, 130

Fourteenth Amendment (US Constitution), 125–126

France, H1N1 response in, 42

Fraudulent scientific articles, 85

Free Exercise Clause, US Constitution, 125

Free radicals, 93

Frey, Sharon, 42

G

Gardasil, 128, 130

See also Human papillomaviruses

Gastroenteritis, 130

GBS (Guillain-Barre Syndrome), 43, 47

General Medical Council (UK), 85

Genital warts and lesions, 112, 128

German measles. *See* Rubella

Germany, diphtheria in, 48

Ghana, 49

Girard, Marc, 42

Girls and women. *See* Cervical cancer; Human papillomaviruses; Pregnant women

GlaxoSmithKline (pharmaceutical), 113

Global Polio Eradication Initiative (GPEI), 15, 29–30

Gostin, Lawrence O., 137

Government Accounting Office (GAO), 54

Group Health Research Center, 63

Guillain-Barre Syndrome (GBS), 43, 47

H

H1N1 virus, 41, 61, 118–119, 120, 160–162

Haemophilus influenzae type b *(Hib)*, 27, 31, 55, 56, 77, 92

Hand washing, 67–68

Hart, Betsy, 137

Health and Healing (Weil), 45

Health care, access to, 113, 154–155

Health-care workers
    mandatory vaccination for, 117–120, 141–144
    as pressuring parents to vaccinate, 90
    vaccination rates, 67–68

"Healthy user" effect, 64

Hepatitis A, 102

Hepatitis B, 35–36, 55, 90–91

Herd immunity, 25–26, 77, 80–81, 87, 95–96, 106–107, 118, 132

Hib (Haemophilus influenzae type b), 27, 31, 55, 56, 77, 92

HiBTiter vaccine, 56

HIV/AIDS, 48–49, 148, 151–155

Hodge, James G., Jr., 137

Home School Legal Defense Association, 121, 125, 126–127

Homeschooling, 125, 127

Horovitz, Len, 72

Human adenoviruses, 148

Human papillomaviruses (HPV)
    adverse reactions to vaccination, 129–130
    cervical cancer and, 75–76, 112–113
    differences from other vaccinations, 132, 134–135
    duration of vaccine immunity, 130–131
    exemption from vaccination, 138–139
    mandatory vaccination against, 128–129, 135–136, 139–140
    opposition to vaccination, 114–116
    target population for vaccination, 94, 114

I

Immune suppression, 93–95

Immune system
    naturally vs. artificially acquired immunity, 24–25, 92–92
    overview, 19–20, 23–24

Immunity duration, 44, 91–92, 94, 97, 130–131

Immunization Safety Review Committee (IOM), 79
Immunogens, 147–148
India, tuberculosis in, 48
Infants
   of hepatitis B-infected mothers, 36
   immunity transfer to, 98
   pertussis effects on, 32
   rubella effects on, 33–34
Infectious disease
   alternate prevention measures, 67–68
   defined, 22
   eradication of, 14–16, 27, 29–30, 82, 106, 111, 146, 149
   fear of and vaccination rates, 75
   international travel and, 30, 37, 76
   non-vaccination and outbreaks of, 72, 77
   sanitation and, 45, 57, 89
Inflammation, 22
Influenza and influenza-like illness
   alternate prevention measures, 67–68
   deaths from, 40, 45, 64, 65–66, 91, 142, 144
   health-care worker vaccination, 117–120, 141–144
   pandemics, 60–61, 90, 156–159, 160–162
   public policy and vaccination, 61–62
   Spanish flu epidemic (1918-1919), 40, 157–158
   swine flu, 40–41, 46–47, 58–59, 61, 118–120 160–162
   vaccination and mortality rates, 62–66
   vaccine delivery, 149
   vaccine development and seasonal mutations, 50, 59–60, 161
   vaccine efficacy, 66–67, 69
Inhaled vaccines, 149
Innate immunity, 19–20
Institute of Medicine (IOM), 52, 79
International travel and infectious disease, 30, 37, 76, 107, 158, 161, 162
Internet, medical information on, 76
Intravenous drug users and tetanus, 38
Intussusception, 130
Iowa, exemptions to mandatory vaccination in, 126

J

Jackson, Lisa, 63–65
Jacobson v. Massachusetts (1905), 102, 132–135
Japan, pertussis epidemic in, 25, 32–33
Jefferson, Tom, 43–44, 63
Jenner, Edward, 71, 132
Jenner Institute, University of Oxford, 150
Jewish communities, 39

L

The Lancet, 71, 83–86
Leishmaniasis, 146
Liberty Clause, US Constitution, 125
Life, statistical value of, 157–158

Live recombinant vaccines, 147–148

Live viruses in vaccines, 47, 92–93, 95, 123, 147–148

Liver disease, 35

Lymphocytes, 20

M

Majumdar, Sumit, 65–66, 67

Malaria, 146, 148, 150

Mandatory vaccination
    of health-care workers, 117–120, 141–144
    history of, 129, 132–134
    for human papillomavirus, 135–136, 139–140
    as necessary for public health, 108–109
    parents' rights and, 122, 137–138
    school entry and, 102–103, 115, 134–136
    voluntary vs., 118, 144

Mandatory vaccination exemptions
    for health-care workers, 143
    for medical reasons, 109
    parents' rights and, 125–127
    for personal beliefs, 104–105, 109–110
    for religious beliefs, 109, 110, 124–125
    state laws on, 102–103, 104–105, 109, 122, 124, 126, 143

Markel, Howard, 68

Mass media, 161

McDonald, Larry, 46

Measles
    elimination of, 106
    infants and, 98
    international travel and, 76
    live viruses in MMR vaccine, 93
    mandatory vaccination and, 134
    outbreaks of, 106–108, 110
    vaccination and reduction of, 30–31, 89
    See also MMR (measles, mumps, rubella) vaccine

Medical profession
    dogmas about vaccination, 51–52, 54, 57
    endorsement of HPV vaccination, 114
    scare tactics of, 90
    See also Health-care workers

MedImmune (pharmaceutical), 58

Mendelsohn, Robert, 45

Meningitis, 27, 31, 33, 80, 92, 93, 94

Merck (pharmaceutical), 113–114, 129, 138

Mercury in vaccines, 42–43, 92

Mexico, H1N1 virus in, 68, 162

Microbes, immune system reaction to, 23–24

Mill, John Stuart, 141

Miller, Neil Z., 88–89

Miscarriage of pregnancy, 34, 39

MMR (measles, mumps, rubella) vaccine, 39, 71, 92–93, 94–95, 98

Mortality rates. *See* Death rates

Mumps, 38–39, 76
    See also MMR (measles, mumps, rubella) vaccine

Mutation of viruses, 16, 43, 60, 93

N

National Childhood Vaccine Injury Compensation Program, 121
National Health Interview Survey, 38
National Institute of Allergy and Infectious Diseases, 62–63, 66
National Institutes of Health, 66, 99, 162
National Vaccine Information Center, 74, 126
National Vaccine Injury Compensation Program, 87, 121, 122
Naturally acquired immunity, 24
New South Wales (Australia), 143
New York State, mandatory vaccination in, 117–118
Nigeria, polio in, 15–16, 30
Non-specific immunity, 19–20
Nutrition and infectious disease, 89–90

O

Offit, Paul, 72–73, 74, 82, 85–86
Ofstead, C.L., 143
Oman, polio in, 48
"On US Preparations for 2009 H1N1 Influenza" (President's Council of Advisors on Science and Technology), 41
Opt-out provisions. See Mandatory vaccination exemptions
Ott, True, 47

P

Pandemics
    AIDS, 151
    defined, 60, 156
    flu, 60–61, 90, 156–159, 160–162
    nutrition and, 90
    public health efforts against, 46–47, 61–62, 67–68
    See also Epidemics
Parents
    informed decision making about vaccines, 79–80
    mandatory vaccination and rights of, 125–127, 137–138
    refusal of vaccinations, 57, 72–74
    See also Children; Mandatory vaccination exemptions
Patch application of vaccines, 149
Pathogens, 19, 20
Paul, Ron, 46
Pediatric Infectious Diseases Society, 104
Pertussis
    death rates, 89
    incidence of, 27, 31–33
    non-vaccination and outbreaks, 25
    outbreaks of, 107–108, 110
    vaccine failure, 48, 96
Pestivirus, 99
Phagocytes, 20
Pharmaceutical industry
    adverse event reporting requirements, 129–130
    liability waivers, 47
    lobbying activity, 129, 138
    vaccine contamination, 98–99
    vaccine manufacturing programs, 60, 161
    See also Clinical trials
The Pink Book (CDC), 53
Placebo-controlled studies, 54–55
Pneumococcal vaccine, 33

Pneumonia, 30, 31, 94
Poland, G.A., 143
Police powers of the state, 133–134, 137
Polio
    death rates, 89
    elimination of, 26–27
    eradication campaign, 14–16, 29–30, 106, 111–112
    vaccination as causing disease, 16, 48, 73, 95, 123
    vaccine contamination, 15, 98–99
Pregnant women
    chickenpox severity in, 34
    H1N1 vaccine, 119
    hepatitis B, 90
    miscarriage of pregnancy, 34, 39
    rubella, 34, 97
Presidents Council of Advisors on Science and Technology, 41, 61
Public health policy
    AIDS prevention, 155
    epidemics and breakdowns in, 37
    flu pandemics, 46, 61–62, 157–159, 160–162
    HPV vaccine, 115–116, 129, 131, 136, 139–140
    mandatory vaccination, 57, 108–109, 126, 133–134, 141–144
    mandatory vaccination exemptions, 72, 104–105, 109–110
    Supreme Court decisions, 102, 132–135
    vaccines as promoting, 25
    See also Centers for Disease Control

Public schools and mandatory vaccination, 102–103, 105, 108–109, 114–115, 129, 132–136
Public trust in vaccination, 15–16, 72, 136–138

Q

Quarantine, 67, 68, 107, 158

R

Religious/personal beliefs and vaccination exemption, 104–105, 109–110, 124–125
Re-vaccination, 44, 91–92, 94, 97
Risks of vaccination, 54–55, 57, 74, 77–79, 82–83, 110
    See also Adverse events
Rotashield vaccine, 130
Rotavirus, 28, 83, 130
Rubella, 33–34, 76, 97, 106
    See also MMR (measles, mumps, rubella) vaccine

S

Sabin, Albert, 111
Salk, Jonas, 49, 111
Sanitation, infectious disease and, 45, 57, 89, 126
School entry and mandatory vaccination, 102–103, 105, 108–109, 114–115, 129, 132–136
    See also Mandatory vaccination
Scientific articles, fraudulent, 85
Sebelius, Kathleen, 41–42
Senior citizens. *See* The elderly

Sexually transmitted diseases, 76, 115–116, 131, 135–136, 137
Shingles, 27–28, 102
SIDS (sudden infant death syndrome), 55, 121
Simonsen, Lone, 64
Sinclair, Ian, 47–48
Smallpox
as caused by vaccination, 47
eradication of, 14, 26, 106
live vs. recombinant virus in vaccine, 147–148
mandatory vaccination and, 102, 132–134
vaccination against as causing AIDS, 48–49
vaccine history, 71
vaccine stability and eradication of, 149
Social distancing, 67
Society for Adolescent Medicine, 114
Soviet bloc countries, diphtheria in, 37
Spanish flu pandemic (1918–1920), 40, 60, 156, 157–158
Specific immunity, 20–21, 43–44
State laws on vaccination exemption, 102–103, 104–105, 109, 122, 124, 126, 143
Statistical value of life, 157–158
Sudden infant death syndrome (SIDS), 55, 121
Supreme Court, US, 102, 132–135
SV-40 (virus), 15, 98–99
Sweden, pertussis in, 48
Swine flu
of 1976, 46–47, 156
of 2009, 40–41, 58–59, 61, 160–162

T
T Cells, 20–21
Tamiflu, 58, 158–159
See also Antiviral drugs
Task Force on Community Preventive Services, 109
Temperature and storage of vaccines, 149–150
Tenpenny, Sherri, 44
Tetanus vaccine, 37–38, 76, 92, 94, 134–135
Thailand, clinical trials in, 152
Tuberculosis vaccine, 48
Tucker, S.J., 143

U
United Kingdom
autism in, 53
H1N1 response, 43, 68
pertussis in, 32, 48
Wakefield article and vaccination rates in, 83–85, 107–108
United States
1976 mass-immunization program, 46
antiviral supply, 159
Constitution, 125
Universities, vaccines required by, 94–95
Unvaccinated individuals
differences between vaccinated and, 63–64
risks to self and community, 77, 80–81
spread of disease and, 103, 106–108
tetanus and, 38

See also Herd immunity; Mandatory vaccination exemptions

V

Vaccination and vaccines
adverse events and, 53, 55, 76, 79, 83, 122–123, 129–130
booster vaccines, 44, 91–92, 94, 97
as cause of targeted disease, 47, 73
contamination of, 15, 98–100
deaths and neurological disorders resulting from, 46
delivery techniques, 148–149
effectiveness of, 56–57, 97
failure rates, 48, 96–97
fear of, 71–74
future of, 146–150
historic importance of, 111
history of, 14
immune system effects, 24
misinformation about, 80, 108
safety and risks of, 54–55, 57, 74, 77–79, 82–83, 110
schedule for administration, 73, 97
specific immunity and, 22, 43–44
stockpiling of, 158–159
stopping before eradication, 30, 31, 33, 34, 35
Supreme Court cases, 102, 132–135
temperature and storage of, 149–150
See also Mandatory vaccination; *specific diseases*
Vaccine Adverse Events Reporting System (VAERS), 122–123

Vaccine development
AIDS vaccine challenges, 151–152
dangers of fast-tracking, 42–43, 50
mutations and, 60
new techniques for, 147–148
testing by manufacturers, 123
Vaccine manufacturers. *See* Pharmaceutical industry
"Vaccine-Induced Disease Epidemic Outbreaks" (Ott), 47
Vaccinia virus, 148
Variola virus, 26
See also Smallpox
Virginia Mason Medical Center, 143
Viruses
live viruses in vaccines, 47, 92–93, 95, 123, 147–148
mutations of, 16, 43, 60, 93
sexually transmitted, 115–116
viral fragments in vaccines, 99
Voluntary vs. mandatory vaccination, 118, 144
See also Mandatory vaccination

W

Wakefield, Andrew, 83–86
Water fluoridation, 89
Weil, Andrew, 45
White blood cells, 20, 22
Whooping cough. *See* Pertussis
Wiznitzer, Max, 73
Women and girls. *See* Cervical cancer; Human papillomaviruses; Pregnant women

World Health Organization (WHO)

    AIDS in Africa and, 48–49

    cervical cancer, 113

    influenza vaccination and, 60, 160–161

    polio campaign, 15, 29–30

    smallpox campaign, 26

Z

Zoster virus (shingles), 27–28, 102

Zucht v. King (1922), 102, 134